The Roots and Wings of School Leadership

The Roots and Wings of School Leadership

CHERYL A. DUNKLE

LEAD+
LEARN
PRESS

ENGLEWOOD, COLORADO

The Leadership and Learning Center
317 Inverness Way South, Suite 150
Englewood, Colorado 80112
Phone 1.866.399.6019 | Fax 303.504.9417
www.LeadandLearn.com

Copyright © 2012 The Leadership and Learning Center
All rights reserved.

Published by Lead + Learn Press, a division of Houghton Mifflin Harcourt.

Note: Every attempt was made to obtain permission for reprint/use of contributors' work. No part of this publication may be reproduced, stored in a retrieval system, or transmitted in any form or by any means, electronic, mechanical, photocopying, recording, scanning, or otherwise, except as permitted by law, without the prior written permission of the publisher.

Limited Reproduction Permission: Permission is hereby granted to the purchaser of this book to reproduce the forms for educational and noncommercial use only.

Notice of Liability: The information in this book is distributed on an "as is" basis, without warranty. While every precaution has been taken in the preparation of the book, neither the authors nor Houghton Mifflin Harcourt shall have any liability to any person or entity with respect to any loss or damage caused or alleged to be caused directly or indirectly by the instructions contained in this book.

All Web links in this book are correct as of the publication date but may have become inactive or otherwise modified since that time. If you notice a deactivated or changed link, please notify the publisher and specify the Web link, the book title, and the page number on which the link appears so that corrections may be made in future editions.

Lead + Learn Press also publishes books in a variety of electronic formats. Some content that appears in print may not be available in electronic books.

ISBN 978-1-935588-39-9
Printed in the United States of America

16 15 14 13 12   01 02 03 04 05 06 07

To Jason and Megan,

my two favorite teachers.

Contents

Foreword xi
About the Author xv
Acknowledgments xvii
Preface xix
Introduction xxi

Chapter One
The Learning Leader: Leaders Developing Leaders 1
What Do the Best Do Better? 2
The Mind, Heart, and Soul of a Hopeful Leader 4
Educational Leadership Policy Standards: ISLLC 2008 6
National Association of Elementary School Principals: *Leading Learning Communities*, 2nd Edition 9
National Association of Secondary School Principals: *Breaking Ranks* ... 10
The Institute for Educational Leadership (IEL) Task Force Report 10
Kouzes and Posner: The Truth about Leadership 11
The Wallace Foundation: The School Principal As Leader 12
Linda Lambert: Building Leadership Capacity in Schools 13
Marzano, Waters, and McNulty: School Leadership That Works 14
Douglas Reeves: Assessing Educational Leaders 16
The "So What? Now What?" of School Leadership 17
Key Ideas 19
Questions to Continue This Discussion 20

Chapter Two
The Visionary Leader: Promoting a Shared Vision of Learning 21
Beginning at the Beginning 21
Educational Leadership Policy Standards: ISLLC 2008 22
Elementary 25 24
Vision: Substance or Symbols? 25
Uniting People 28
Are You Convinced Yet? 31
Key Ideas 32
Questions to Continue This Discussion 33

vii

Chapter Three
The Cultural Leader:
Nurturing and Sustaining a Learning Organization ... 35
- What Are We Talking About? ... 36
- Culture or Climate? ... 38
- Healthy or Toxic? ... 41
- Educational Leadership Policy Standards: ISLLC 2008 ... 43
- Elementary 25 ... 45
- A Resource or a Risk? ... 48
- Key Ideas ... 49
- Questions to Continue This Discussion ... 50

Chapter Four
The Resourceful Leader: Managing a Learning System ... 51
- The Ends and the Means ... 53
- Leadership *or* Management ... 54
- Leadership *and* Management ... 55
- Total Quality Management ... 58
- Educational Leadership Policy Standards: ISLLC 2008 ... 59
- Elementary 25 ... 62
- Key Ideas ... 65
- Questions to Continue This Discussion ... 66

Chapter Five
The Collaborative Leader: Partnering for the Benefit of Learning ... 67
- Professional Learning Communities ... 69
- Can Collaboration Be Taught? ... 70
- Getting Smarter Together ... 72
- Data Teams ... 75
- Motivation Theory ... 77
- Educational Leadership Policy Standards: ISLLC 2008 ... 80
- Elementary 25 ... 81
- Key Ideas ... 83
- Questions to Continue This Discussion ... 84

Chapter Six
The Ethical Leader: Leading with Integrity 85
    The Resurgence of Character Education in Our Schools 87
    Moral Imperatives: Beyond Compliance to Commitment 88
    Educational Leadership Policy Standards: ISLLC 2008 89
    Servant Leadership 91
    Ethical Dimensions of School Leadership 94
    Elementary 25 96
    Key Ideas 98
    Questions to Continue This Discussion 99

Chapter Seven
The Change Leader: Advocating for All Learners 101
    Facing Some Hard Facts 104
    What Is Resiliency? 107
    Theories on Change 108
    Educational Leadership Policy Standards: ISLLC 2008 112
    Common Core State Standards:
        From Common Sense to Common Practice 113
    Elementary 25 115
    Keys Ideas 116
    Questions to Continue This Discussion 117

References and Suggested Reading 119
Index 129

Foreword

Jason B. Dunkle, Ph.D.

Excellence in educational leadership might best be defined as an abstract "mix" of talents and skills that, when applied in a school setting, accomplishes the most important outcome—improved student learning. Never are all of the talents and skills necessary for leadership success naturally found in a single person, and each educational leader I have encountered in my career has had a somewhat different "mix." Certainly, school leadership is not simply a list of skills that can be defined and learned like a high school student memorizing the quadratic formula or conjugating the Spanish verb *aprender*. The talent—the ability to apply knowledge and adapt to situations—is equally as important. Really, all great leaders should be constantly trying to improve their own "mix" of talents and skills to become most effective in their roles within the school.

As a high school golf coach, I have the privilege of working with many talented young golfers. I have realized over the years that I can't teach talent. But what I can do is use the successes and failures I have personally experienced as a golfer to establish a set of ideals that I believe should be shared to mentor any young golfer to reach his full potential. These concepts from personal experience paired with tidbits about golf I have picked up from reading books, as well as from watching and listening to other golfers tell about their own experiences with the game, form a solid body of understanding that can be helpful to the aspiring golfer. *The Roots and Wings of School Leadership* is written in exactly the same tradition. Cheryl Dunkle has clearly defined the role of a school leader, and her own experiences and accumulated knowledge provide keys to success that should be shared with all of those interested, so continual improvement in school leadership is the norm. This book is not simply theory. Cheryl explains how her understanding of school leadership worked in practice—in the creation of a new (and wildly successful) elementary school in Douglas County School District in Colorado.

One who wants to improve his leadership effectiveness can be coached, much like the golfers on my team—given hints, strategies, and, frankly, just thought-provoking ideas that stretch and maximize that combination of skills and talents in an effort to support a person reaching their full potential. Cheryl, my mother and mentor in my own role as an educator, has demonstrated to me over her 45-year career, and my comparatively short educational career of 20 years, that the great educational leader (and really any excellent educator) constantly strives to improve. Undoubtedly, the best leaders reflect on their own strengths and weaknesses, and then work to make any weaknesses their strengths. In this book, Cheryl shares those beliefs and practices that she has acquired during her own career that can help any educational leader stretch his own talents and knowledge ... to achieve that stronger "mix."

The title of this work is no accident. The "roots" are those educational ideals that provide the strong foundation on which to build for the future. Cheryl's understanding of the "roots" comes from a thorough meta-analysis of the current best thinking in educational leadership. *The Roots and Wings of School Leadership* organizes the ideas of the strongest thought partners in educational leadership and puts forth a coherent explanation of key considerations about the roles of the school leader. Cheryl also explores the "wings"—those emerging ideas on best practices in educational leadership that will allow school leaders and students to "fly." Cheryl creates these "wings" as she challenges the reader to take the best thinking and ask questions about how to practically implement these suggestions to improve learning in schools. Cheryl successfully shares her thoughts to create seven key categories that best define the role of the school administrator. The 21st-century school leader must be visionary, resourceful, and a steward of continuous learning. In addition, he must be ethical, collaborative, and the creator of a learning culture within the classroom and the school. But, the one characteristic of the modern educational leader that best characterizes the spirit of this book is the "change leader." Education is in a constant state of flux, and the strong leader must be able to predict, adapt, and lead in change that equates to the best opportunities for learners. This book is about that change, and how an enhanced understanding of the role of the school leader can lead to change for the better.

Know that when you read this work, you are reading the thoughts of one of the finest. Cheryl's commitment to excellence in education is unsurpassed. Her collected knowledge about the educational leader is an unmatchable amalgamation of extensive experience and dedicated research. She has been an inspiration to many; her own talents and skills in school leadership have touched and enhanced the work of hundreds of teachers, and, in turn (and more importantly), tens of thousands of students. Read this work! Take Cheryl Dunkle's thoughts on the educational leader and create for yourself a stronger, personal "mix" of skills and talents; be the school leader the teachers, the parents, and (most importantly) the students need and deserve.

Jason B. Dunkle, Ph.D.
Denver, Colorado

About the Author

Cheryl Dunkle is a Professional Development Associate with The Leadership and Learning Center in Englewood, Colorado, working with educators across the country in the areas of assessment, accountability, and standards implementation. She was a practicing elementary school principal with Colorado's Douglas County School District from 1983 to 2001. Prior to that, Cheryl served as an elementary school guidance counselor and a teacher of primary students for 14 years. She retired from public education in July 2001.

In addition to her leadership in public schools, Cheryl has taught for several colleges and universities both online and in the classroom, and has coordinated a cohort teacher education program in the Denver metro area. Cheryl has a wealth of experience with professional development, including work as a district "trainer of trainers" in the areas of early childhood education, effective teaching strategies, group facilitation, Cognitive Coaching, student discipline, and techniques for success in working with parents. She has extensive knowledge in adult development and learning theory, as well as standards-based education and data-driven decision making. Her current area of study and interest is investigating elements of successful implementation of the Common Core State Standards.

Cheryl has been named a National Distinguished Principal by the National Association of Elementary School Principals, is a past president of the Colorado Association of Elementary School Principals and recipient of their department service award, was a member of the coordinating council for the Colorado Association of School Executives, and was the planning principal for a new elementary school in Douglas County. She gained invaluable knowledge and skills about teaching, learning, and leadership through each of these challenging and rewarding experiences.

Cheryl lives with her husband, Wayne, in Castle Rock, Colorado, close to her two adult children, Jason and Megan, both of whom are teachers. She enjoys spending time with her four grandchildren, as well as reading, writing, and gardening in her spare time. She can be reached at 303.504.9312, ext. 506, or through her e-mail address at cdunkle@leadandlearn.com.

Acknowledgments

As a leader, you realize that people always come first. Any success in learning and in life can be attributed to what people choose to do with what they have. This book illustrates the amazing potential of ideas, inspiration, and imagination joined together with passionate people to collectively accomplish great things. It is not surprising, then, that I have many people to thank for sharing their time and talent with me during my 45-year career as a teacher and a leader. *The Roots and Wings of School Leadership* represents the tremendous possibilities that exist when collaboration, conversation, and commitment are focused and then freed to create a learning community that is incredibly special. I owe a great debt of gratitude to some remarkable colleagues who have enriched my professional and personal life and confirmed my belief that people have the power to move right past what *is* in order to embrace what *can be*.

The Douglas County School District Elementary No. 25 core planning team has always had a special place in my educator's heart of hearts. That is why their presence and impact is felt on every page of this book. During the work of planning for a new school in a fast-growing Colorado community, the members of that team displayed vision and wisdom far beyond my own. Thank you Rachelle Amo, Mary Ann Gabriel, Jan Olearnick, Linda Shingleton, Sally Foster, Judy Nelson, and Carla Randall. And a special thanks to Carol Gardner, who saw what I saw and thought what I thought about teaching and learning during timeless reflections on her front porch.

The Leadership and Learning Center has had an enormous influence on my thinking as a school leader. The things that we research and write about, the topics we discuss, and the issues we care deeply about are important to so many hardworking and invested teachers and principals across our nation and, in fact, around the world. We try to make our ideas about teaching, learning, and leadership more coherent and compelling, and I think we succeed. My appreciation to Kristin Anderson, Katie Stoddard, Laura Besser, Cathy Lassiter, Angela Peery, Mary Jane O'Connell, Julie Smith, Lisa Almeida, Aimee Corrigan, Jo Peters, Al Thompson, Ainsley Rose, and Lillian Hawkins for helping me connect my thoughts to the right work and giving me the confidence to share them with others. And, of course, an enormous thank you to Doug Reeves, who leads us all with the skillfulness of a general and the integrity of a judge. He intuitively and consistently embodies all of the good that this leadership book is about.

And finally, to all of my students, young and not so young, who have kept me engaged in intelligent thought about education for so long, I humbly say thank you. I have rehearsed my ideas with you, responded to your questions, and then reflected on your answers together with mine. You offered me the opportunity to become a member in the club of educators I respect and admire so much described in the first chapter of this book. "Youthful maturity" continues to be a goal that I work toward each and every day, and your respect and kindness help me meet it.

Preface

I collect quotes. In the past, I kept folders and folders of them to include in school newsletters, to liven up faculty meetings, to use as an activator in seminars, and to introduce my college courses. Now, in the digital age, I bookmark favorites on my computer. Mark Twain is one author and humorist who is well represented in my stash. During the writing of this book, I repeatedly referred to his common sense and effortless brilliance for grounding and inspiration. So I have incorporated several of his famous sayings, not as arbitrary embellishments or window dressings for the chapters, but to provide deliberate clarity for the information, ideas, and thoughts included in them.

The first of my many Mark Twain quotes is a challenge to me as an author to demonstrate respect for you as the reader. "I didn't have time to write a short letter, so I wrote a long one instead" indicates to me that I have an obligation to discover the right word, the most apt phrase or sentence, in order to share my beliefs and experiences as a school leader in the most economical and efficient way possible. I should not waste your valuable time by making you hunt for meaning. People in the business of leading schools are busy folks who do not have the luxury of casually breezing through text. So my first commitment to you is to be brief and to the point when provoking your reflection on the seven chapters of this book.

Second, Twain reminds us that "Facts are stubborn, but statistics are more pliable." My goal for this book is to provide evidence-based practices and quality standards for performance that school leaders need to understand and implement to support and sustain the learning communities they serve. The findings and conclusions of the most highly recognized and regarded research partners in school leadership are offered for your consideration. The references and suggested reading listed at the end of the book are indicators of the thoroughness of my investigation and also of my dedication to providing factual information about how to effectively lead learning organizations.

One of my favorite Twain quotes is, "If you hold a cat by the tail you learn things you cannot learn any other way." It reminds us that authentic experiences provide a relevance and coherence to our discovery of new perceptions and points of view. Our beliefs, values, and resultant actions are filtered through a similar "cat memory" that everyone can relate to. I promise that *The Roots and Wings of School Leadership* will be a practical guide, and perhaps can help you avoid some of the pitfalls of leadership that could divert and potentially derail your journey to success.

The seven chapters in this book do not represent any innovative quick fixes or shortcut solutions for improving schools. My experience as a building leader is that there aren't any. No single person, program, practice, or policy guarantees success in educational reform. There are, however, consistent and deeply held beliefs and values aligned with deliberate adult actions that research, theory, and common sense acknowledge are essential elements in the work of creating and leading great schools. Each of the references I investigated cites very similar content in terms of evidence-based strategies for bold and inspired leadership in any context.

A book like this, and there are thousands of them out there, must inspire a passionate and hopeful picture of the future, one that everyone sees as desirable and, most important, possible. Again, Twain nails this sentiment: "You can't depend on your eyes when your imagination is out of focus." Visionary school leaders provide the focus and direction that invite participation in creating this shared "north star" for our work. My intention is to illustrate with the passion of a zealot how schools can become what we need them to be for our students' and our nation's future.

Thank you for choosing this book as a potential addition to your expanding leadership collection, by the way.

Introduction

The *Roots and Wings of School Leadership* is my attempt to describe, analyze, challenge, and sometimes reconstruct some prevalent standards and provocative ideas for school leadership. These chapters describe the results of my personal use of inquiry to frame some problems and gather evidence-based solutions. The structure of the book is organized around the framework of the *Educational Leadership Policy Standards: ISLLC 2008*, an update by the Council of Chief State School Officers of the school leadership standards developed in 1996 by the Interstate School Leader Licensure Consortium. This platform gives us a common set of high-level policy standards that are universally recognized and accepted to launch our conversation about each of the six standards and leadership functions. Hopefully, the following chapters will entice you to assertively test some of your assumptions and to generate some big ideas and essential questions of your own, and will engage you and your colleagues in some thought-provoking debates about the imperative work of school leaders.

Chapter One
The Learning Leader: Leaders Developing Leaders

Schools are special places that have entrusted their potential for success to dedicated, talented, and compassionate leaders. Engaging the mind, heart, and soul, school leaders set the direction and priorities to focus the immense and urgent work of quality teaching and learning.

ISLLC 2008 asserts that leadership standards must:
- reflect the centrality of student learning.
- acknowledge the changing role of the school leader.
- recognize the collaborative nature of school leadership.
- improve the quality of the profession.

- inform performance-based systems of assessment and evaluation for school leaders.
- demonstrate integration and coherence.
- advance access, opportunity, and empowerment for all members of the school community.

Source: Adapted from Council of Chief State School Officers, 2008

These universal leadership features of skillful participation, vision, inquiry, collaboration, reflection, and student achievement all interact to create the new responsibilities of collaborative leadership. An abundance of research about school improvement suggests that these elements are essential to initiating and sustaining school reform efforts. Chapter One introduces common sets of beliefs and behaviors of dynamic school leaders who are successful in cultivating a shared vision of excellence in teaching and learning for everyone.

Chapter Two
The Visionary Leader: Promoting a Shared Vision of Learning

This book idea evolved when I was a practicing principal selected to become the planning principal for a new elementary school in my district. At that time, there were no prototypes, no strategic plans, and no operating manuals to guide the work of opening a new school. However, I did have my incomplete but vivid dreams of how to define, design, and develop a new place for learning: one that would create an inclusive community of learners; a high-performance culture for students and adults; a coherent and rigorous standards-based curriculum; and finally, an environment where moral and ethical behavior was the norm. The story of the creation of Elementary No. 25 represents that journey and introduces the perplexing and complicated question, "Can everyone lead?"

Our hopes and dreams—the "wings" of school leadership—lift us up to do more than we ever thought possible to fulfill the moral imperative of providing an excellent education for all of our students. They support the proclamation of our collective vision and act as catalysts for becoming whom we need to become to foster and shape the focus, courage, and energy needed to accomplish the purposes of a learning organization. Chapter Two deals with the vital leadership function of creating a shared vision for a brighter educational future for our students and families.

Chapter Three
The Cultural Leader:
Nurturing and Sustaining a Learning Organization

I realize with a deep appreciation and an overwhelming sense of awe that the incredible opportunity I had to lead the creation of a learning community from its basic beginnings is not the reality for most school leaders. But I also believe that the insights, understandings, and skills gained from that experience can translate into guiding the transformation of a mediocre school into a great one, and, more dramatically, into leading a revolution of changed outlook and expectations to turn around a failing school.

The foundational principles for establishing relationships between people and ideas in a school are among the "roots" of school leadership. They can energize or undermine. If the school culture is a strong and positive one, amazing learning occurs that is significant, continuous, and widespread for both the adults and the students. Chapter Three introduces characteristics of a vibrant school culture that embodies core values and the belief that everyone can learn and reach a very high level of performance and accomplishment.

Chapter Four
The Resourceful Leader: Managing a Learning System

Debates about the distinction between managing a school and leading one have always existed. Creating systemic organizational patterns and structures to fit a learning purpose is, for me, an essential consideration. How to use time wisely; how to acquire the necessary human resources, materials, and services to benefit and support students; how to organize for effective instruction; how to integrate technology into the effort; and how to guarantee a safe and secure learning environment fall on the management side of school leadership. There is nothing on this list that can be eliminated or discounted as less important than other functions of leadership.

This important responsibility of managing and being accountable for a powerful learning system is another part of the "roots" of school leadership, and skillfulness in this area of leadership is a very visible sign of effectiveness and efficiency. Chapter Four investigates some of the foundational components that describe the "running" of a school.

Chapter Five
The Collaborative Leader: Partnering for the Benefit of Learning

Building an inclusive learning community that invites everyone to come together to promote and communicate high standards for learning is a vital responsibility of school leaders. Welcoming people with diverse opinions and ideas and encouraging them to share their vision of educational excellence respects the significance of each contribution from students, teachers, parents, and the greater community and adds a richness to the universal purpose of schooling.

The power of this partnership is the topic of study in Chapter Five. The more skillful school leaders are at bringing key players to the table to thoughtfully challenge the status quo of student and adult performance, the more dramatically those performances will improve. Leaders are required to guide professional learning communities to collectively formulate accurate and honest conclusions about how they are doing. It is a leadership behavior that demands trust, respect, finesse, imagination, and vision. Fostering a collaborative effort in pursuing the school community's goals for improvement involves both the "roots" and the "wings" of school leadership, because partnering often requires a shift in a school's foundational considerations, and it also allows for a more expansive vision for the future.

Chapter Six
The Ethical Leader: Leading with Integrity

Accountability for results requires that school leaders be transparent and open about the specific successes and challenges that their learning communities experience. Good leaders champion the deep and honest examination of cause and effect data for the sole purpose of everyone getting better at what they do in support of continuous school improvement. They discover and promote the shared values and beliefs that benefit the common good for all members of their school community.

Chapter Six discusses the critical relationship between moral and ethical behavior and the credibility a school leader establishes to garner the required trust to lead others. Integrity is another essential part of the "roots" of school leadership. If the members of the school community trust and respect the leaders of the school enough that they are willing to share their time, talent, energy, enthusiasm, intelligence, creativity, and commitment, the goal of school improvement is not so elusive and difficult to achieve.

Chapter Seven
The Change Leader: Advocating for All Learners

Within the current educational context of the K–12 Common Core State Standards in English language arts and mathematics, the Common Core's anchor standards for college and career readiness, and next-generation assessments, a school leader acts as a change agent. Connecting and expanding opportunities for all students to have access to high-quality learning opportunities is an authentic and relevant function of a school leader. Today's reality is that there are too many students not graduating from high school, or if they do graduate, they are potentially unprepared for the demands of college or a career. We are falling behind our international peers in the global marketplace, and to eliminate that divide, school leaders have the obligation to focus on what matters most: the quality of daily instructional interaction in each classroom between each teacher and each student.

Promoting the best outcome for every learner certainly implies that we must look to the future with an optimistic and hopeful sense of the possibilities and also with the courage to initiate and support the necessary changes to reach that future. Our capacity as leaders to do this represents the "wings" of school leadership. Chapter Seven celebrates this leadership challenge to be a simultaneously reflective and resilient advocate for the diverse needs of all students.

My invitation to you, and possibly Mark Twain's challenge to you as well, is to become
- a learning leader,
- a visionary leader,
- a cultural leader,
- a resourceful leader,
- a collaborative leader,
- an ethical leader, and
- a change leader.

Our students, present and future, deserve nothing less.

CHAPTER ONE

The Learning Leader: Leaders Developing Leaders

"There are basically two types of people. People who accomplish things and people who claim to accomplish things. The first group is less crowded."

MARK TWAIN

Rarely do you meet an "old" educator. What I mean by that statement is directly related not to the number of birthdays people have celebrated, but instead to my experiences with retired school people who actively create incredible richness in their daily lives and immeasurably enhance the lives of others around them. They do not waste their time or talent, nor do they lack temerity. What they pack into each and every day is remarkably bold and brave.

I have had the privilege of knowing many teachers and administrators who are now in their 70s, 80s, and even 90s. These dynamic people are still traveling to exotic places, white-water rafting, biking, and trekking in the mountains of Colorado, and they are using smart phones and tablet computers to stay in touch. There is not an apathetic or lethargic bone in their bodies, and their wisdom and compassionate insight continue to be sought out by people searching for a sensible solution to the world's problems. What does this phenomenon of "youthful maturity" have to do with the issues of current school leadership? A lot.

I have thought deeply about why these forever young-thinking and -behaving individuals are so different from their contemporaries who are constantly complaining about their aches and pains and their boredom, and who are pessimistically analyzing all of the opposing perspectives around them rather than focusing on the unifying premises that are more pervasive and promising. I think I have discovered some answers that will engage us all in hopeful and productive conversations about the power and importance of our current work in education.

What Do the Best Do Better?

First, and most obvious, these great teachers and principals that I am adulating have had the opportunity to spend their entire professional careers hanging out with young people who challenged and stretched them to see the future with uncompromised hope and optimism. There is something special about spending extended time in schools that ignites us and moves us to amplify our strengths, to confidently communicate and model our beliefs and values, and, as a result, to confront ideas alongside our students. Both businessman Robert Half and author Robert Heinlein are credited with saying, "When one teaches, two learn." No matter who said it, this sense of inquiry and discovery to use our minds well keeps us young.

Second, schools are not only intellectual places that grow our minds, but also social places where adults and students feel safe and inspired to share ideas, emotions, and aspirations that grow our hearts. Trust emerges when people who believe and care about what *you* believe and care about surround and protect you, yet also challenge you to expand your perspectives about how the world is supposed to work. A sense of belonging evolves when learners, both adult and student, feel significant and competent in the eyes of their peers. There is genuine appreciation for the contributions they make when they are present and a sense of loss when they are absent. Relationships keep us engaged and young.

Last, and most important, schools are typically moral places that provide and promote a culture of purpose and meaning that empowers us to perform beyond our potential, to become an important part of something larger than ourselves. Schools grow our souls. As explorer, author, and filmmaker Sir Laurens van der Post remarked, "We have to turn inwards, to look into ourselves; look into this container which is our soul; look and listen to it." This process begins with creating wonderment and contemplating desirable and possible futures and ends with an inclusive, genuine, and authentic commitment to appeal to the common good that exists in everyone and to inspire them to envision and create something better than what currently exists. The moral aspect of schooling is often labeled "vision," and the effective stewardship of a vision keeps us hopeful and future-oriented. Again, it grows our souls.

Why are these passionate elder educators so vital to the current study of school leadership? I have come to realize that they have spent dedicated time deliberately developing their minds, their hearts, and their souls to a greater degree than others. They continue to be intellectually, emotionally, and morally connected to a higher purpose—one of service—that is just as compelling and irresistible today as it was when they were actively leading a learning community. They feel an obligation to share and spread hopeful optimism. Today's world deserves no less, and probably needs this capacity to be a strong and capable leader even more now than it did in previous generations.

What would these creative and committed sages remind us to think about as we head to our schools each day? I think that they would bolster our spirits by reinforcing how critically important our work is right now to the future of our nation and how we must collaborate with each other to accomplish the incredibly challenging tasks that lie ahead for school leaders. So we will begin our conversation about what the best school leaders do better by discussing the minds, hearts, and souls of these amazing individuals.

The Mind, Heart, and Soul of a Hopeful Leader

Two esteemed colleagues and longtime friends met me at a coffee shop early one summer morning a few years ago to reminisce about our challenging and stimulating work as planning principals for new elementary schools in our district. When we began our task, there were no guidelines about how to open a new school. But each of us had definite ideas about how to create an inclusive community of learners, a high-performing culture for students and adults, a coherent and rigorous standards-based curriculum, and an environment where moral and ethical behavior was the norm. Our collective thoughts ultimately provided me with the impetus to write this book on school leadership.

The mind of a talented leader has an unquenchable thirst to learn and understand. Effective leaders are tenacious and single-minded in creating a community of learners. As the leader grows and discovers, so does each individual in the organization, because knowledge is shared, not private. Good leaders know what they know, they know what they don't know, and they relentlessly pursue resources to achieve excellence. They are thoughtful and reflective educators who inspire inquiry and debate. Leading from the mind produces a purposeful and focused learning community of hope.

When operating from the heart, leaders passionately lead from the inside out. The leaders' core beliefs and values quickly become transparent and visible to the entire school community through their words and actions. People always come first, before programs, practices, and policies. Good leaders care deeply about every individual, both adults and children. Leading from the heart engages all to take risks, to push boundaries, and to do whatever it takes to positively impact the lives they touch. Leading from the heart creates a joyful place of hope.

When a leader's heart and mind converge, one leads with soul. The soul of leadership connects the artful and skillful leader's ability to navigate and balance between the mind and the heart. While the heart strives for harmony and acceptance, the mind creates cognitive dissonance and a healthy challenge to the status quo. The person who leads with soul is able to both ignite and direct the passion necessary to form a community focused on excellence and equity for all. Our image of "soul" is of something elusive and invisible, but it can still be secured in the mind, and most certainly be felt in the heart. The soul of leadership can inspire hope that is limitless.

A leader who acts with mind, heart, and soul is one who learns from reflections about the past and plans for the future, and who keeps the faces of those affected planted at the center of the vision. Therein lie the "roots" and "wings" of school leadership.

Revering the mind, heart, and soul of leadership reveals my personal passion and professional pride for what we do in support of teaching, learning, and leading in these amazing places called schools. We should consider it a privilege to spend time here influencing the future and making an obvious difference in the present. Because schools are complex places facing some of the most inherently difficult challenges the world offers, it takes much more than technical expertise as a leader to solve the problems, puzzles, and contradictions that reside here. It requires hope.

I am hopeful, but not naïve. Hope is not a leadership strategy. It is a belief, an attitude, or a disposition; it is a critical part of our character that we embrace and enjoy in large or small doses based upon our experiences. It is an essential ingredient that motivates us to change our behaviors to reflect the shared vision of what the future can be. But again, hope is not a leadership strategy and the stakes are too high in today's school reform efforts to continue to rely on hope alone. We need research-based leadership practices to bolster our optimism so that we can support all students in reaching their highest potential for learning and life. Leadership standards help identify priorities, so that appropriate actions can be taken to continue and enhance this crucial work.

The good news is that we have many sets of high-quality standards from which to choose. The following sections provide an overview of some of the most widely recognized and comprehensive standards and ideas about leadership in the United States.

Educational Leadership Policy Standards: ISLLC 2008

The educational landscape over the past 30 years in particular has shown us that reluctant or obligatory compliance is not enough to address the current dilemmas we face in our schools. The prolonged periods of status quo and stagnation highlighted in the 1983 publication of *A Nation at Risk* (National Commission on Excellence in Education) portrayed a dismal state of affairs in our public schools. The call for reform rang loudly across our nation and led to a standards-based system for students, but not for adults. All of the mandates and potential sanctions from the No Child Left Behind Act for low-performing schools did little to inspire us to work harder. We were already working as hard as we could. I would often hear, after feeling a bit discouraged or disillusioned, the words: "Take heart, we are doing all that we can."

To help us "take heart," the standards set by the Interstate School Leaders Licensure Consortium (ISLLC) in 1996 affirmed the beliefs that defined what an effective principal should know and be able to do to lead this reform effort. At the time, those standards were the most widely used and accepted set of guidelines for determining whether or not a principal was effective. In fact, 35 states adopted the 1996 ISLLC standards as the state standards for school principals and eight additional states used them as templates and models for creating their own standards.

A revised version of those 1996 standards, *Educational Leadership Policy Standards: ISLLC 2008*, developed by the Council of Chief State School Officers with the help of the Wallace Foundation, represents the latest set of high-level policy standards for education leadership. This document provides guidance and direction to state policymakers as they work to improve education leadership preparation, licensure, evaluation, and professional development. Adopted by the National Policy Board for Educational Administration (NPBEA), these standards reflect the wealth of new information and lessons learned about education leadership over the past decade.

These revised standards have been updated to reflect today's educational concerns, although they are similar in structure to the original ISLLC standards. *Educational Leadership Policy Standards: ISLLC 2008*, like the 1996 standards, stress that a school leader's first and foremost job is to improve learning for all students, and that the way to accomplish this task is by improving teaching. Because the 1996 standards were widely used to inform leadership policy decisions, the 2008 standards are more directly policy-oriented (Council of Chief State School Officers, 2008). They organize the functions that replaced the knowledge, skills, and dispositions that were stated in the six 1996 standards and help to define strong school leadership relative to those six standards. The standards in the *ISLLC 2008* document are often referred to as the "de facto" national leadership standards because of their extensive visibility and pervasive use in all of our states. These standards represent the broad, high-priority themes that education leaders must address in order to promote the success of every student.

ISLLC 2008 requires effective school leaders to:
- facilitate the development, articulation, implementation, and stewardship of a vision of learning that is shared and supported by all stakeholders.
- advocate, nurture, and sustain a school culture and instructional program conducive to student learning and staff professional growth.
- ensure management of the organization, operation, and resources for a safe, efficient, and effective learning environment.
- collaborate with faculty and community members, responding to diverse community interests and needs, and mobilizing community resources.
- act with integrity and fairness, and in an ethical manner.
- understand, respond to, and influence the political, social, economic, legal, and cultural contexts.

The team revising the 1996 standards used the following lofty and challenging principles during their development of the *ISLLC 2008* policy standards to refocus the work of school leadership. Their aim for the revised standards was that they would:
- reflect the centrality of student learning.
- acknowledge the changing role of the school leader.
- recognize the collaborative nature of school leadership.
- improve the quality of the profession.
- inform performance-based systems of assessment and evaluation for school leaders.
- demonstrate integration and coherence.
- advance access, opportunity, and empowerment for all members of the school community.

Source: Adapted from Council of Chief State School Officers, 2008

National Association of Elementary School Principals: *Leading Learning Communities*, 2nd Edition

The year 2008 was a prolific year for revisions to established school leadership standards, and the magic number of standards seemed to be six. In addition to the highly acclaimed *ISLLC 2008* policy standards on school leadership, the National Association of Elementary School Principals (NAESP) also provided us with revised content, tools, and resources for principals to meet their individual learning goals and to support their work with learning communities in *Leading Learning Communities: Standards for What Principals Should Know and Be Able To Do* (2008a).

> NAESP states that effective leaders of learning communities:
> - lead schools in a way that places student and adult learning at the center.
> - set high expectations for the academic, social, emotional, and physical development of all students.
> - demand content and instruction that ensure student achievement of agreed-upon standards.
> - create a culture of continuous learning for adults tied to student learning and other school goals.
> - manage data and knowledge to inform decisions and measure progress of student, adult, and school performance.
> - actively engage the community to create shared responsibility for student performance and development.
>
> Source: Adapted from National Association of Elementary School Principals, 2008a

National Association of Secondary School Principals: *Breaking Ranks*

Both middle and high school administrators seek guidance from *Breaking Ranks II: Strategies for Leading High School Reform* (2004) and its associated series of professional learning opportunities from the National Association of Secondary School Principals (NASSP). Listed below are the recommended 10 skills for successful school leaders that have been assembled from the experiences of effective school leaders at both levels.

The 10 skills that represent the majority of what school leadership entails:

- Setting instructional direction
- Teamwork
- Sensitivity
- Judgment
- Results orientation
- Organizational ability
- Oral communication
- Written communication
- Developing others
- Understanding your own strengths and weaknesses

Source: Adapted from http://www.nassp.org

The Institute for Educational Leadership (IEL) Task Force Report

The Institute for Educational Leadership's task force on principalship declares that the top priority of principalship must be leadership for learning. The task force's report, *Leadership for Student Learning: Reinventing the Principalship* (2000), specifies three key roles that the principals of the 21st century should fulfill:

- Instructional leadership that focuses on strengthening teaching and learning, professional development, data-driven decision making, and accountability
- Community leadership manifested in a big-picture awareness of the school's role in society; shared leadership among educators, community partners, and residents; close relations with parents and others; and advocacy for school capacity building and resources
- Visionary leadership that demonstrates energy, commitment, entrepreneurial spirit, values, and conviction that all children will learn at high levels, as well as inspiring others with this vision both inside and outside the school building

Source: Adapted from Institute for Educational Leadership, 2000

Kouzes and Posner: The Truth about Leadership

James Kouzes and Barry Posner (2010) suggest 10 fundamental and enduring truths about leaders' beliefs and behaviors based upon more than 30 years of study with more than a million research subjects:

- Leadership begins when you believe you can make a profound difference in the lives of those you serve.
- Others need to believe in what you stand for and what you represent to willingly follow your lead.
- Leaders need to align personal values and organizational demands by requesting a shared commitment to both.
- Leaders must offer an exciting vision of the future that followers can embrace and work toward.
- Leadership discovers talent and supports its development for the benefit of the individual and the entire organization.

- Trust is the glue that holds individuals and teams together.
- Challenge and change are always associated with great achievement.
- Leaders are willing to do anything that they ask others to do.
- Learning is the master skill of leadership and requires time, practice, feedback, and coaching.
- Love of the people, the mission, and the work motivates a leader to invest what it takes to transform a system.

Source: Adapted from Kouzes and Posner, 2010

The Wallace Foundation: The School Principal As Leader

The Wallace Foundation has issued more than 70 research reports on the impact of school leadership since 2000, and suggests that effective principals perform five key functions. They lead by:

- shaping a vision of academic success for all students—one based on high standards.
- creating a climate hospitable to education in order that safety, a cooperative spirit, and other foundations of fruitful interaction prevail.
- cultivating leadership in others so that teachers and other adults assume their part in realizing the school vision.
- improving instruction to enable teachers to teach at their best and students to learn at their utmost.
- managing people, data, and processes to foster school improvement.

Source: Adapted from The Wallace Foundation, 2012

Linda Lambert:
Building Leadership Capacity in Schools

Linda Lambert (2002) defines leadership capacity as "broad-based, skillful participation in the work of leadership. In schools with high leadership capacity, learning and instructional leadership become fused into professional practice." Schools with this capacity have some important features in common:

- Principal and teachers, as well as many parents and students, participate together as mutual learners and leaders in study groups, action research teams, vertical learning communities, and learning-focused staff meetings.

- Shared vision results in program coherence. Participants reflect on their core values and weave those values into a shared vision to which all can commit themselves. All members of the community continually ask, "How does this instructional practice connect to our vision?"

- Inquiry-based use of information guides decisions and practice. Generating shared knowledge becomes the energy force of the school. Teachers, principal, students, and parents examine data to find answers and to pose new questions. Together they reflect, discuss, analyze, plan, and act.

- Roles and actions reflect broad involvement, collaboration, and collective responsibility. Participants engage in collaborative work across grade levels through reflection, dialogue, and inquiry. This work creates the sense that "I share responsibly for the learning of all students and adults in the school."

- Reflective practice consistently leads to innovation. Reflection enables participants to consider and reconsider how they do things, which leads to new and better ways.

Participants reflect through journaling, coaching, dialogue, networking, and their own thought processes.

- Student achievement is high or steadily improving. "Student achievement" in the context of leadership capacity is much broader than test scores; it includes self-knowledge, social maturity, personal resiliency, and civic development. It also requires attention to closing the gap in achievement among diverse groups of students by gender, race, ethnicity, and socioeconomic status.

Source: Adapted from Lambert, 2002

Marzano, Waters, and McNulty: School Leadership That Works

In 2005, McREL (Mid-continent Research for Education and Learning) researchers Robert Marzano, Tim Waters, and Brian McNulty recorded in their book, *School Leadership That Works* the largest-ever examination of quantitative research on the impact of school leadership on student achievement. McREL researchers also conducted an exhaustive review of leadership literature to help practitioners understand how to apply the results of this examination to their practices. Key findings from this integrated examination of research of leadership led to the 21 leadership responsibilities that statistically are directly and substantially related to higher student achievement.

- **Culture:** Leader fosters shared beliefs, a sense of community, and cooperation. Effect size .29

- **Order:** Leader establishes a set of standard operating procedures and routines. Effect size .26

- **Discipline:** Leader protects teachers from issues and influences that would detract from their teaching time or focus. Effect size .24

- **Resources:** Leader provides teachers with materials and professional development necessary for the successful execution of their jobs. Effect size .26

- **Curriculum, instruction, assessment:** Leader is directly involved in the design and implementation of curriculum, instruction, and assessment practices. Effect size .16

- **Focus:** Leader establishes clear goals and keeps those goals in the forefront of the school's attention. Effect size .24

- **Knowledge of curriculum:** Leader is knowledgeable about current curriculum, instruction, and assessment practices. Effect size .24

- **Visibility:** Leader has quality contact and interactions with teachers and students. Effect size .16

- **Contingent rewards:** Leader recognizes individual accomplishments. Effect size .15

- **Communication:** Leader establishes strong lines of communication with teachers and among students. Effect size .23

- **Outreach:** Leader is an advocate and spokesperson for the school to all stakeholders. Effect size .28

- **Input:** Leader involves teachers in the design and implementation of important decisions and policies. Effect size .30

- **Affirmation:** Leader recognizes and celebrates school accomplishments and acknowledges failures. Effect size .25

- **Relationships:** Leader demonstrates an awareness of the personal aspects of teachers and staff. Effect size .19

- **Change agent:** Leader is willing to actively challenge the status quo. Effect size .30

- **Optimizer:** Leader inspires and leads new and challenging innovations. Effect size .20
- **Ideals/beliefs:** Leader communicates and operates from strong ideals and beliefs about schooling. Effect size .25
- **Monitors/evaluates:** Leader monitors the effectiveness of school practices and the practices' impact on student learning. Effect size .28
- **Flexibility:** Leader adapts his or her leadership behavior to the needs of the current situation and is comfortable with dissent. Effect size .22
- **Situational awareness:** Leader is aware of the details and undercurrents in the running of the school and uses this information to address current and potential problems. Effect size .33
- **Intellectual stimulation:** Leader ensures that faculty and staff are aware of the most current theories and practices and makes the discussion of these a regular aspect of the school's culture. Effect size .32

Source: Adapted from Marzano, Waters, and McNulty, 2005

Douglas Reeves: Assessing Educational Leaders

And finally, perhaps one of the most comprehensive lists of leadership behaviors can be found in the second edition of *Assessing Educational Leaders* (2009a) by Douglas Reeves. In this evaluation resource, suggested domains of leadership are offered with three caveats. Leadership evaluators must ask: "Is this domain within the direct control or influence of the leader?" "Is this domain directly related to the school's mission and vision?" and "Is this domain subject to objective description so that the people responsible for evaluating the leader have a clear and consistent understanding of what successful leadership in this domain really means?"

Reeves' recommended potential leadership domains are:
- Resilience
- Personal behavior
- Student achievement
- Decision making
- Communication
- Faculty development
- Leadership development
- Time, task, and project management
- Technology
- Learning

Source: Adapted from Reeves, 2009a

The "So What? Now What?" of School Leadership

In-depth conversations about the importance of school leadership to student success are long overdue. To diligently and with unwavering determination define and describe what masterful school leaders do on a daily basis in their schools and with their learning communities to positively influence student learning is a necessary next step in education reform. There is no excuse for us to delay. The preponderance of evidence indicates that school leadership is second only to teaching as a school-related influence on student learning. The highly regarded and referenced research report issued by the Universities of Minnesota and Toronto (Leithwood, et al., 2004) validates that we need to get this leadership thing right or our students and schools will suffer as a result of our lack of clarity and indecisiveness.

The prevalence of these rigorous standards and compelling ideas about school leadership allows us to explore the multidimensional and intricate aspects of this highly complex topic. We need to reach consensus on the most important beliefs and actions of preK–12 leaders in achieving the desired goals of improved teaching and learning in America's schools. With this common language about school leadership and the agreed-upon standards for performance, we can begin to describe, observe, and measure these structural pillars of a solid education system for all students. It truly is an exciting time to dig deep into the implications and study of our work. These features of skillful participation, vision, inquiry, collaboration, and reflection are all attached to higher student achievement and they connect and intersect to create the new tasks of shared leadership. An abundance of research into school improvement suggests that these leadership responsibilities are vital to the school reform process.

So what would my "youthfully mature" friends, whom I introduced at the beginning of this chapter, have to say about all of this? They would probably first ask why this discussion took so long to initiate. Time is fleeting. It is obvious from each of the cited references, even with a cursory view, that there is more agreement than dissention about what a great leader genuinely believes and consistently does as a result of those beliefs. My guess is that those veteran educators would not be shy or tentative about giving the following advice with passion and presence:

- Be bold and brave, with advocacy for school leadership as a vital cornerstone of educational reform.
- Be clear on the actions of leaders that matter most and directly contribute to student success.
- Lead from the heart, mind, and soul; the work requires nothing less.
- Be truthful, honest, and transparent about where we are and where we need to be with our school improvement efforts.

- Create and communicate a shared vision of the desired and possible future of education.
- Establish and nurture a caring and compassionate school culture where everyone feels valued and respected as a contributing member of the learning community.
- Manage the resources necessary for an effective and efficient learning system.
- Collaborate with every stakeholder to ensure that learning excellence and equity are available to all students.
- Lead with integrity and a moral compass that defines what behavior is ethical and just.
- Use our experience and our influence to make the world a better place.

Let's roll up our sleeves and get to work.

Key Ideas

- We need to capitalize on the attitude of "when one teaches, two learn" and extend it to the zest for life that retired educators typically display.
- Schools are intellectual places that allow us to use our minds well.
- Schools are social places that develop a sense of significance and competence and a feeling of belonging.
- Schools are moral places that promote a culture of purpose and meaning that empowers us to embrace causes that are bigger than ourselves.
- Revering the heart, mind, and soul of a leader reveals the personal passion and professional pride we deeply feel working in schools for the benefit of our students.

- The six *Educational Leadership Policy Standards: ISLLC 2008* (Council of Chief State School Officers, 2008) are the de facto national leadership standards that support school leaders in promoting the success of every student.
- There is much research-based agreement about what school leadership is and how potentially powerful it is in accomplishing the work of improved learning for students and adults.

Questions to Continue This Discussion

- Describe people you know well who have dedicated their entire lives to spending time teaching and learning with students. Are they the vital human beings that were introduced at the beginning of this chapter?
- Author and educator Thomas Sergiovanni states, "School effectiveness requires authentic leadership. … Leaders with character ground their picture in purposes and ideas that define the schools they serve as special places and then act with courage and conviction to advance and defend these ideas" (2000). How do you become an authentic leader?
- What is your top-10 list of leadership beliefs and behaviors that are essential to the work of school reform?
- What personal and professional differences have you made that have had a positive impact on your school community?
- What more needs to be done?

CHAPTER TWO

The Visionary Leader: Promoting a Shared Vision of Learning

"Don't part with your illusions. When they are gone, you may still exist, but you have ceased to live."

MARK TWAIN

Beginning at the Beginning

With this little book I've tried hard to make one big point: that effective school leadership matters tremendously in raising student achievement, improving the total quality of our public school system, and elevating the educational experience for everyone. Chapter One reminded us that research supports that an effective principal in every school is second only to an effective teacher in every classroom to impact and influence high student achievement. This knowledge requires a shift in thinking away from the idea that managing orderly learning environments where teachers work autonomously with their classroom doors closed is the main responsibility of school leadership. Now we know that helping to create an open and accessible inclusive community where a shared vision, goals, and commitments to excellence in teaching and learning are honored and executed is the main function of a powerful school leader. Margaret Wheatley and Myron Kellner-Rogers (1996) say it best: "We can no longer stand at the end of something we visualize in detail and plan backwards from that future. Instead we must stand at the beginning, clear in our mind, with a willingness to be involved in discovery ... it asks that we participate rather than plan." What a wonderful reminder that collaboration is key to ensuring that everyone who is invested in that future has an opportunity to create a shared vision of it.

This chapter begins at the beginning with the study of how school leaders create, communicate, nurture, and sustain a vision that can be owned and shared by everyone who has an interest and investment in the outcome of increased learning for all. This initial work requires answering the foundational and powerfully personal question, "Why do schools exist?" *Educational Leadership Policy Standards: ISLLC 2008* affirms the basic importance of this obligation and responsibility of school leadership by placing it first among the six standards.

Educational Leadership Policy Standards: ISLLC 2008

School leaders engage their communities in the development of a shared vision of student learning. This statement articulates what we desire to accomplish as a learning community and guides our collective actions to give focus and meaning to what we believe about teaching and learning. Leaders align the necessary resources, both human and material, to support the priorities of that vision and they are responsible for communicating it within and beyond the school.

Standard 1: An education leader promotes the success of every student by facilitating the development, articulation, implementation, and stewardship of a vision of learning that is shared and supported by all stakeholders.

Functions:
- Collaboratively develop and implement a shared vision and mission.
- Collect and use data to identify goals, assess organizational effectiveness, and promote organizational learning.
- Create and implement plans to achieve goals.
- Promote continuous and sustainable improvement.
- Monitor and evaluate progress and revise plans.

Source: Council of Chief State School Officers, 2008

Logically, in order to improve the current state of education, we must first dream about the desired state. It is an opportunity for us to describe in detail what the ideal could be without constraints. That dream or imagined ideal becomes our north star, our steady guide and vision of the future that propels us toward clarifying our purpose and motivating us to perform beyond our resources and even our potential; our "wings" of school leadership, if you will. As Peter Senge (2006) says, "A shared vision is not an idea, but a force in people's hearts." That is powerful stuff in any organization, but it is a major reason that most educational leadership standards pay close attention to the vision-building process as an indispensible component of leading a school.

If promoting the success of every student is our primary leadership responsibility, then having a clear and comprehensive picture of what that success looks like, sounds like, and feels like is essential. Great visionary leaders challenge the status quo with words that are vivid and yet concrete. School leaders who possess this vision think deeply about how to stimulate thought and reflective discussion that results in establishing a shared and common vision about the moral purpose of schooling. Leading by example, they display behaviors that honor the broader view, that acknowledge different perspectives, and that deliberately shape and guide this valuable collaboration through dialogue. They help build the capacity of the adults to see the limitless possibilities generated by bold thinking and courageous action.

Whether you are charged with transforming an average school into an exemplary one, turning around a broken school, or beginning at the beginning with a new learning community, visionary leadership supersedes all other leadership tasks. If you don't have an end in mind, it will be impossible to determine where you should begin. By definition, vision implies the future, and that future can inevitably garner feelings of uncertainty, resistance to change, and fear of the demands of the unknown. It is the visionary leader's task to dispel that angst by building trust that a new way is possible and that the support for reaching this desired and shared future will be ample and consistently available throughout the entire journey.

Elementary 25

I have believed for a very long time that better schools lead to a better world. When I had the opportunity to invite nine extremely talented and passionate educators to discuss and debate if there was a better way to accomplish the work of teaching and learning in a rapidly growing community in Colorado, I did not hesitate. Accepting the challenge of opening a new elementary school in my district seemed to be the next logical step on my career path. An incredible journey of self-discovery, both personally and professionally, began with my acceptance of this new leadership responsibility. It resulted in shaping and being shaped by the creation of a powerful learning community that represented the collective wisdom of many invested individuals, a truly once-in-a-lifetime experience.

One of the most poignant affirmations I received as a school leader during that nine-month adventure was that the anatomy of leadership begins with the leader's heart, the hopeful and truthful heart that remains visible and vulnerable to everyone through words and actions. It is not the leader's head or intellect that answers the surface question, "What do we do now?" as one might imagine, and it is not the leader's hands that accomplish the daily work that responds to the practical question, "How do we get it done?" as some might expect. The essential question, the one that should be asked and answered first is, "Why do we do what we do?" As educator Roland Barth stated in *Learning by Heart* (2001), "To put it simply, in addition to a brain, we have a heart, and we want to put it to use in promoting young people's learning. Exclude this vital organ from our work, and you get compliance at best." So to follow Barth's wise advice, we must explore vision building through the heart of a leader first.

Vision: Substance or Symbols?

Sadly, vision statements are a dime a dozen and as a result can become trite and tired. Writing a vision statement is a topic on hundreds of thousands of Web sites. We are constantly searching for value-laden words that communicate how to create a better future, and we might end up visiting one of those Web sites for inspiration and ideas. But a vision statement is much more than fancy-font words collected on a glossy poster board to hang in a prominent place in the school office. Business and management researcher Jim Collins (2001) said, "There is a very big difference between being an organization with a vision statement and becoming a truly visionary organization. The difference lies in creating alignment to preserve an organization's core values, to reinforce its purpose, and to stimulate continued progress towards its aspirations."

That alignment that Collins alluded to was the reason for many late Tuesday nights for the core leadership planning team for Elementary 25. We spent an inordinate amount of time and energy creating our vision statement and reaching agreement on the common language and common meaning of our sentiments. We accomplished this by initially answering many of the "why do we exist?" questions that we proposed to each other and then to the entire learning community. To name a few:

- For what purpose are we creating this community of learners?
- What do we stand for as educators? What are our unwavering beliefs about students, teaching, and learning?
- What do we want our students to know and to be able to do proficiently, and most important, who do we want our students to become?
- How do we want our students to think and reason?
- How do we want everyone to live their lives together in this school? How will everyone care for each other, help each other, and respect each other?
- What will our obligations be to each other?
- How will we share the responsibilities of leadership in this school?

- How will parents and the greater community become partners with us?
- How will we measure and communicate success and how will we be personally accountable to this vision of success with generous investments of our time and talents?
- How will we get better at what we do for our students?

These questions, which took a great deal of time to craft and then answer, served us well as a planning team. They not only were important in defining what our desired future should be, but they also defined who we were as a collective faculty. When it came time to invite others to join Elementary 25, we used many of these anchor questions as the basis for our interview process. We learned quickly that when we are surrounded by people who thrive as idea makers, who believe what we believe but challenge us to explore unique and creative solutions, and who encourage us and pick us up when we stumble, we have the foundation of a trusting and protective culture. That culture supports the necessary risk taking that discovery and deep learning require. It abates the fear and uncertainty of the personal changes that are innate in exploring anything new.

When our stakeholders requested that we consider a change in policy or procedure, we could refer to our animated discussions about these essential questions to determine an authentic and aligned reply. When resources became tight, we could use these responses to determine our priorities. When it was time to create and implement strategic plans to achieve our goals and promote continuous and sustainable improvement, these "why do we exist" questions provided the data to focus our efforts on the right work. As a result, we were more efficient and more productive in following through on our plans to improve student learning. The planning team realized that the initial work we did to translate our beliefs and our shared values about excellence and equity in educational opportunities into a compelling vision was time very well spent.

Uniting People

Douglas Reeves states in *The Learning Leader* (2006), "The first obligations of leadership are articulating a compelling vision and linking clear standards of action that will accomplish the vision. This approach applies to tasks small and large, from respecting the time of colleagues by starting and ending meetings on time to keeping commitments and meeting goals. Success is not an ephemeral concept, but it is clearly described. Every team member knows every day what the word 'success' means and how it has been achieved."

Not only does the vision need to be compelling and clear, as Reeves suggests, but also shared and owned by all of the stakeholders. It unites people and provides one of the most significant and powerful intrinsic motivators for action. It is based upon data that inform where the organization is currently and where it is stretching to go. The leader becomes an architect of the future with a feasible blueprint or strategic plan that is comprehensive and detailed enough to move everyone from a blurry dream to a realistic picture of what can and should be.

The planning team at Elementary 25 progressed through the typical stages of unclear and abstract emotional statements of purpose to more concrete and finite reflections of our beliefs and values about education that could be measured and could provide genuine accountability for our work with students. The closer we came to those specific actions, the more excited we became. We wanted the challenge of success to be visible and accessible as well as inspirational. We wanted to have definable goals that all of the stakeholders could identify with and help us attain.

Everyone is seeking meaning and purpose beyond themselves, especially educators, who have a deeper sense of mission than most. I have never met any school leaders who do not passionately believe they can make a dramatic difference in the lives of children. Visionary leaders believe they can change the future and create ideal images and graphic pictures of what a school can become. They clearly see this place in their minds and hear the busy sounds of eager children and enthusiastic adults as if they already exist. Then through quiet persuasion, or loud cheerleading, they invite others into their vision of the future—the "wings" of the learning organization.

I found that Ernest Boyer's book *The Basic School* (1995) gave form, structure, and conceptual integrity to my ideas and vision. I recommend this wonderful resource to anyone who is in a position to revisit some basic assumptions about schooling. I don't know if Dr. Boyer's plan was to offer this valuable support deliberately, but in my discussions with many principals across the country who needed a framework for thinking about the ingredients of a successful standards-based school, this book is still mentioned as a hallmark resource. Our interpretation at Elementary 25 of what Dr. Boyer was asking us to do was that he recommended creating community through cooperation and collaboration. His book suggests that we cultivate character through self-discovery, that we construct climate through caring and consideration, and that we connect curricula, instruction, and assessment through thoughtful practice. I used this as my road map for the trip of a lifetime, and I cannot emphasize enough how profoundly the power and relevance of his thinking for creating or transforming a school still resonates with me. The nearly two decades since that book's publication have not changed our vision or our obligation to our students to provide excellence and equity in teaching and learning. In fact, I believe that vision and obligation have strengthened over time.

When speaking about the concept of vision, many people get hung up with terms and definitions. Are we speaking of a mission, a vision, a belief statement, a core value statement, or a school philosophy? My experience confirms that as long as your stakeholders have a common understanding about the terminology and its shared meaning, you can label your conversations and resulting work any way you wish.

The guiding questions that were mentioned in the "Vision: Substance or Symbols?" section of this chapter will guarantee a rich and engaging dialogue about a vision, a mission, or a belief statement about the work of creating or improving schools. Building a statement that evokes pride, purpose, identity, and passion is the goal of this exercise. The statement generally develops over months of reflecting and refining and then is formalized in writing in less than 20 minutes. At least, that was our experience at Elementary 25. It represents the heart and soul of the group and challenges and stretches individuals to become part of a dynamic and resilient learning community.

Both the delight and the difficulty of this daunting task stem from the fact that we are rarely asked to think about our craft and the purpose for our work. Time for research and reexamination is a luxury for most professionals. I invite anyone who has a school leadership role to engage or reengage in this vision-building process. Revisiting why we do what we do is certainly not a waste of time, and it promotes a greater sense of purpose and urgency that propels us to do more and do it better. We need to remember that the future of our schools is not just someplace we are going, but a place we are constantly creating. The paths are discovered along the way with people united to a common purpose and shared vision of hope and optimism for our students.

Are You Convinced Yet?

Have these testimonials convinced you yet? Has the value of "facilitating the development, articulation, implementation, and stewardship of a vision of learning that is shared and supported by all stakeholders" resonated with you as a vital leadership standard that is crucial to move an entire educational platform forward? Whether you are responsible for leading the planning for a new building, transforming an average school into a better one, or turning around a failing school, the impact of a shared vision is remarkable. It requires courageous action on the part of the school leader to initiate the conversations that craft the vision statement, but it takes even more boldness and bravery to champion the stewardship of that vision. Holding people accountable to achieve what represents the best thinking and the ideals of the entire community is not all happiness and light. Tension caused by the difference between the desired state and the current reality can be a source of amazing creativity and imagination, and can also represent diverse perspectives about success that challenge us.

But if we can all imagine a school where

- eager students run, walk, and ride to school to discover, learn, and make connections to how the real world works,
- eager students enter an attractive and "kid-friendly" building that welcomes them each and every morning,
- eager students learn from talented staff members who know their craft and love to spend most of their daylight hours with their charges,
- eager students understand the "why" of learning as well as the "what" and the "how,"
- eager students treat each other with care and compassion, appreciating everyone's ideas and contributions,

- eager students are encouraged to try new learning on for size and are congratulated for their attempts,
- eager students are supported by active and involved families who recognize and appreciate the significance of a quality standards-based education,
- eager students are allowed to show what they know and can do in authentic situations, and
- eager students consistently perform at their highest potential and realize success daily,

...that shared vision can move us closer to what we dream and hope for our children.

Whether you are a parent, a community member, a business leader, a school board member, or a professional educator, your wish is for this imaginary school to exist just up the block in your neighborhood. If you are reading the pages of this chapter, you already have a strong desire to contribute in some capacity to the creation of this perfect learning place and watch with vigilance as it transforms the lives of children and adults. In order to participate in this grand endeavor you must be a dreamer, a planner, a doer, an inspirer, a believer, and, most of all, a visionary leader.

Key Ideas

- A vision features a compelling picture or image of what a school can become in the future. It is feasible and attainable.
- A shared vision is connected to the entire learning community and articulates intrinsic values and hopes that everyone deeply holds for the future.
- A shared vision needs to be translated into actions and plans that can and will be implemented.

- A shared vision needs to be nurtured and used. It serves as the filter for all of the decision making that is vital for teaching and learning success.

Questions to Continue This Discussion

- How are shared visions created, communicated, and nurtured in your school community?
- How do shared visions become the blueprint of a school? How can their presence influence every action taken and every decision that is made on behalf of the students?
- Why are the "why do we exist" questions so potent and powerful in establishing purpose and meaning for the work that school leaders do?
- How do we as leaders keep the vision fresh and vital in the minds of all of our stakeholders?

CHAPTER THREE

The Cultural Leader: Nurturing and Sustaining a Learning Organization

"Climate is what we expect. Weather is what we get."

MARK TWAIN

Walk into any reputed outstanding school and you discover almost immediately that you have entered a very special place. The buzz of excited, enthusiastic, and engaged learners, the broad smiles of professionally confident and competent adults, and the vibrant sense of promise that emanates from both students and staff welcomes every guest into an important enterprise. Everyone here stands tall and proud and moves with direction and purpose. Observers recognize and appreciate the pervasive feeling and tone of positive energy. This is a cursory description of the evidence of a healthy school culture or school climate—the topic of this critical leadership chapter.

As a principal, I took great pride when visitors would stop me in the hallways and tell me how "good" the school felt, but I didn't give that subjective comment much thought until researching what that "good" feeling really meant to the work that was being accomplished there. After extensive reading and reflection, I know to pay much more focused attention to the quality and character of daily school life, as it tells us much about the potential for realizing success for students and the prospect of encountering motivated and productive adults.

So, here we go again, discussing yet another elusive and abstract concept found in educational environments: how a school feels to the internal and external partners in teaching and learning. School cultures, like school visions, imply subtle and intangible meanings that are sometimes difficult to define and explain. Since they involve behaviors with deep patterns of shared values, beliefs, and traditions, they are pervasive and detectable but challenge us to aptly describe them. Extensive research on school leadership advises that we had better get this phenomenon figured out quickly, since many aspects of a healthy culture are included as critical elements in every research-based study of a high-performing organization.

What Are We Talking About?

Individuals questioning the world around them develop new and tentative theories for coping with that world and, in the process, convince others of the validity and effectiveness of those experimental strategies. Over time, the behaviors that make sense and are useful transfer into widespread lessons learned and become viable mental models of the world, which much later become deeply rooted cultural assumptions. These implicit beliefs are the last to be compromised and sacrificed, and when a forced choice must be made, what remains after that decision is what is perceived as culture.

Another, less cumbersome, way to define culture is a shared set of rules that gives meaning and logic to the world. Those rules include "if/then" statements that confirm a cause-and-effect relationship. If we do this, then that will naturally follow. If we want or need this, then we have to perform that. In time, beliefs about this relationship guide our actions and we see a consistent picture of reality and predictable patterns of behavior. When new evidence comes along that tests our beliefs, we either assimilate it or disregard it based upon what we perceive to be true and right. As an example, if a young child has a scary experience with a frisky puppy, that child assumes that all dogs are suspect until a gentle dog changes the youngster's reality. From that point forward, dogs are acceptable pets and not to be feared. Similarly, as adults, we change our behavior and our adjusted beliefs follow suit. There is great hope in this statement. As leaders, if we provide teachers with a new way to approach a situation, their beliefs about teaching and learning are forever changed.

As long as our beliefs continue to correspond to the realty around us, we move ahead. The challenge occurs when our picture of reality is at odds with what is actually occurring. Rules, structures, rituals, and traditions become less relevant and functional, and a change in behavior is necessary. Since we rarely question, discuss, or reflect upon the cultural implications of our beliefs and assumptions, this mandate for change is often met with initial resistance. Some would prefer to continue with maladaptive responses that might even jeopardize our success rather than investigate a new way of thinking and acting.

School culture has borne the brunt of many excuse-type explanations about why things do not easily or quickly change in education. Many school leaders say, "We can't think about 'x' right now because 'y' is so ingrained in our learning culture." Culture dictates how we are expected to feel and react. When our culture values the weekends rather than the weekdays, teachers who look forward to Monday are suspect. When our cultural priority is "I" instead of "we," collaboration and teamwork are difficult. Our culture establishes who are the heroes and who are the villains, what is achievement and what is failure, what is flexible and what is nonnegotiable, what is a right and what is a responsibility, and how we are to view the world. It is our filter to sort and select what matters to us. It is imperative that we consider the power culture has on school improvement efforts.

Culture or Climate?

The terms "culture" and "climate" have been used interchangeably in many resources addressing the study of school environments. I choose to link them together for the purposes of our discussion, even though each term has layers of distinct meaning attached to it. Both terms have similar characteristics, but "climate" refers to the impressions, feelings, and expectations that are shared by a learning community, whereas "culture" is a much broader expression that goes deeper into the values, beliefs, assumptions, and traditions held sacred by a learning community. Metaphorically, a school culture can be thought of as the school's identity or personality and a school climate represents the daily attitude or mood of a school. Culture is viewed over time and is more permanent. As a result, culture is much more difficult to influence and change. Climate is temporal and more responsive. Both concepts are critical considerations in leading schools (Gruenert, 2008).

Over the last three decades, educators and researchers have worked to identify specific elements that comprise school climate and, in the process, to identify exactly what school climate is. Although there appears to be no one list that summarizes these elements to the satisfaction of everyone, virtually all researchers suggest that there are four major components that are essential to pay attention to: safety, relationships, teaching and learning, and the school environment.

When a school climate is healthy, students and adults feel socially, emotionally, and physically safe. They are engaged in valuable work and respected for their contributions to it. Students, families, and educators work together to create and contribute to a compelling vision of school. Educators model and nurture an attitude that emphasizes an enthusiasm and excitement for rigorous learning. And everyone contributes to the practices of the school that care for the physical environment and nurture the emotional environment (Cohen, 2006).

A widely accepted and often-accessed resource on the topic of school climate and culture is *Shaping School Culture: The Heart of Leadership* (1999) written by Terrence Deal and Kent Peterson. The research conducted by these two highly regarded experts on school culture continues to confirm that a strong and positive learning culture or climate supports many necessary leadership functions, including:

- fostering effort and productivity.
- improving collegial and collaborative activities that in turn promote better communication and problem solving.
- supporting successful change and improvement efforts.
- building commitment and helping students and teachers identify with the school.
- amplifying energy and motivation of staff members and students.
- focusing attention and daily behavior on what is important and valued.

If all of these transparent elements are not sufficient to convince you of the impact of school culture on our leadership work, think about the influences they contribute to our main mission: high student achievement. Deal and Peterson have determined that

- focus (what people pay attention to),
- commitment (how people identify with the school),
- motivation (how hard people work),; and
- productivity (the degree to which people achieve their goals)

all relate to excellence and success and are essential to turning around any low-performing organization or sustaining a high-performing culture. If continually improving our schools is the goal, then these critical components of culture must be at the forefront of our efforts.

Just imagine what a combination of the following characteristics of a healthy school culture would bring to reform initiatives in a troubled school:

- A mission focused on student and teacher learning
- A rich sense of history and purpose
- Core values of collegiality, performance, and improvement that engender quality, achievement, and learning for everyone
- Positive beliefs and assumptions about the potential of students and staff to learn and grow
- A strong professional community that uses knowledge, experience, and research to improve practice
- An informal network that fosters positive communication
- Leadership that balances continuity and improvement
- Rituals and ceremonies that reinforce core cultural values
- Stories that celebrate successes and recognize heroines and heroes
- A physical environment that symbolizes joy and pride
- A widely shared sense of respect and caring for everyone

The keys to what Deal and Peterson (1999) and others have suggested are that whatever we are referring to when we mention the terms culture and climate, we need to recognize as ubiquitous concepts, concepts that go wherever we go. These terms are behind all closed classroom and conference room doors, they exist in the faculty lounge, the main office, and on the entire school campus, and they are underneath and within every conversation and interaction that occurs in the daily life of a school. They are the real source for the "unwritten rules and traditions, norms, and expectations" (Deal and Peterson, 1999, p. 3). This is why culture and climate require constant attention, monitoring, and nurturing. Left uncared for, culture and climate can evolve into negativity, fragmentation, hopelessness, and excuses and finger-pointing for struggling performance. Taken together, culture and climate underlie all that goes on and directly affect our beliefs and assumptions as well as the entire learning community's actions and attitudes.

Healthy or Toxic?

I think we can agree with Deal and Peterson (1999) and many other expert educators that the benefits of creating and sustaining a positive learning environment, a culture of inquiry and thought, and a climate of passion and excitement are obvious and necessary. A school having such characteristics will be a place where students enjoy coming every day, a place where they feel accepted and appreciated, confident in their ability to guide their own learning and behavior, bonded with others who care about their progress and success, empowered and engaged, and intrinsically motivated to accomplish great things. Teachers will feel efficacious and committed, sharing the responsibility for the ambitious learning outcomes and actions of every student with colleagues they admire and respect. Parents will be grateful and work to support this positive learning community, and as a result of the strong culture of excellence, the school will be a source of immense pride for the entire community of stakeholders invested in its success. Culture is foundational, and is a major part of the "roots" of a learning organization.

Ideally, all schools should be safe, fun, intellectually stimulating places where students and adults explore a variety of topics with interest and excitement and work together to realize their hopes and dreams for a brighter future. The reality, however, is that many schools think of themselves as possessing these dynamic traits of a healthy culture and climate when in fact they do not. Pockets of negativity exist where expressions of cynicism, stories about past failures, pessimistic beliefs about the personal power to make a difference, exclusive cliques, and a sense of despair dominate the attitudes and discussions of the members of the organization. These cultures quickly become dysfunctional and unproductive and stay that way until leadership initiates deliberate plans to change them.

Ultimately, improving a school's culture is more of a leadership "must" than an option or a strategy. Michael Fullan (2001) states, "Reculturing is a contact sport that involves hard, labor-intensive work." Roland Barth (2002) asserts, "A school's culture has more influence on life and learning in the schoolhouse than the president of the country, the state department of education, the superintendent, the school board, or even the principal, teachers, and parents can ever have." Shaping the culture, as this effort is sometimes called, requires that leaders foster a climate of commitment to learning as the central mission of schools, encourage collaborative relationships of trust and respect to share the work, create networks that decrease teacher isolation and promote professional learning to stimulate effective teaching practices, monitor and measure what is important, and think of and respond to student needs before considering the convenience of adults. These leadership actions are a very big deal and impact the success of every school improvement effort.

Educational Leadership Policy Standards: ISLLC 2008

ISLLC 2008 recognizes the importance of these leadership tasks to creating and sustaining a school culture in which the primary obligation is ensuring that students have the opportunity to shine as learners. Standard 2 addresses the need to build a learning community and an instructional program that support the success of both students and adults. It emphasizes the shared commitments to high expectations, coherence in practice and policy that provides common frameworks for completing the work, and positive connections to the people involved. School practitioners must be involved in teaching and leading, and organizing schools to be better places for learning.

> **Standard 2:** An education leader promotes the success of every student by advocating, nurturing, and sustaining a school culture and instructional program conducive to student learning and staff professional growth.
>
> **Functions:**
> - Nurture and sustain a culture of collaboration, trust, learning, and high expectations.
> - Create a comprehensive, rigorous, and coherent curricular program.
> - Create a personalized and motivating learning environment for students.
> - Supervise instruction.
> - Develop assessment and accountability systems to monitor student progress.
> - Develop the instructional and leadership capacity of staff.

> - Maximize time spent on quality instruction.
> - Promote the use of the most effective and appropriate technologies to support teaching and learning.
> - Monitor and evaluate the impact of the instructional program.
>
> Source: Council of Chief State School Officers, 2008

As Gary Phillips, founder and president of the National School Improvement Project, concludes, "Positive learning can only take place in a positive culture. A healthy school culture will affect more student and teacher success than any other reform or school improvement effort currently being employed. If people don't improve, programs never will."

Many schools have developed and implemented elaborate school improvement plans based on accountability measures and other curriculum, instruction, and assessment activities. However, there is a realization that these efforts in isolation often fall short of attaining the expected results. Additionally, these efforts often demoralize an already overworked school staff. Research conducted by the Center for Improving School Culture (www.schoolculture.net) in more than 8,200 schools supports the belief that administrators, teachers, and students will not be able to maximize their potential if the culture of the learning community is toxic, no matter what improvement initiative is implemented. Many other independent researchers have found overwhelming correlations between the health of a school's culture and student achievement, staff satisfaction, parent engagement, and community support.

While there is no "one size fits all" culture for classrooms, schools, or school districts, three discrete cultural markers have been identified and measure the pervasive strength of a culture. These markers include professional collaboration, affiliation and collegiality, and self-determination and efficacy.

Elementary 25

Collaboration, affiliation, and efficacy pretty much described the actions and beliefs of students and adults at Elementary 25 on most days. Even though we did not have an existing school culture, the one we worked hard to build was precious to us, and once it was firmly established, we collectively surrounded it and protected it like a newborn baby. It represented who we were as a staff, what was vitally important to us, and how we consistently treated one another in the service of our students.

Our work on culture began with another tried-and-true professional contribution, this one from Jon Saphier and Matthew King written in 1985. "Good Seeds Grow in Strong Cultures" emerged as one of the guiding resources that our planning team constantly referred to when issues of school culture arose. We definitely were planting seeds as a new staff and we were committed to having those seeds grow and develop into the sturdy and beautiful foundation of a great school where teaching and learning flourished. The cultural norms that were introduced decades ago by Saphier and King are as relevant and significant today as they were then. They represent the functional "little black dress or the durable gray suit" that is still in style, still fits, and still makes us feel well dressed and prepared for any occasion. Try these norms on for size and see if you agree that they are still useful and built to last for our current discussions about school culture. Saphier and King recommend that we consider:

- Collegiality
- Experimentation
- High expectations

- Trust and confidence
- Tangible support
- Reaching out to the knowledge base
- Appreciation and recognition
- Caring, celebration, and humor
- Involvement in decision making
- Protection of what's important
- Traditions
- Honest, open communication

No surprises and provocative ideas here, right? We certainly did not find any at the time we were collaboratively creating the culture of Elementary 25, but the work of holding each other accountable for these norms was more challenging. We worked hard to honor each of these ideas and the result was a high level of trust and respect that overcame most obstacles, disputes, and debates, and kept us grounded and always looking forward. I encourage you to resurrect this article from the archives and read it with renewed attention to the impact of each norm on your growth and success as a school community and to reestablish the "roots" of a good school culture.

Compare and contrast these twelve norms with a contemporary list of climate considerations created by the National Center for Urban School Transformation (2011):

- Leaders establish high expectations for everyone's involvement. Leaders expect everyone to behave in ways that respect and value everyone else in the organization. Expectations are high, yet reasonable. Leaders model those expectations daily. They fairly, assertively, and respectfully address issues when individuals fail to meet those expectations.

- Leaders value improvement and growth. Teachers, parents,

and students feel like they can take risks and try to improve because they know their efforts will be appreciated and supported. Professional development is not an event; it is a culture that pervades the school. People are constantly learning to improve their contributions to student success.

- Leaders keep conversations constructive. Leaders refuse to be passive when others choose to be negative. Respectfully, but clearly, administrators and teacher leaders speak out when others claim that goals are unattainable. Leaders use research and data to focus on opportunities to improve, not on reasons to blame.

- Leaders keep attention focused on the impact of everyday efforts on students. Leaders communicate frequently, consistently, and in multiple formats to convey the impact of everyday school actions on student lives.

- Leaders promote ambitious goals that generate enthusiasm and build a sense of mission. Leaders push beyond compliance and encourage everyone to embrace goals that will make a difference in students' lives. People commit to goals they see as worth their effort.

- Leaders build hope. Leaders give students, parents, teachers, and support staff reasons to believe that their efforts are worthwhile. College and careers are constant topics of focus. Policies are designed and implemented to nurture, sustain, and rekindle hope.

- Leaders celebrate progress frequently. Leaders celebrate improvements both formally and informally. They find elements of success worth celebrating in results others see as failure. They are skillful at acknowledging everyone who contributed to successes.

- Leaders build leaders. Leaders create platforms for the leadership of many others—teachers, parents, and students—who want to influence school improvement. Leaders maximize opportunities for input from others and distribute leadership opportunities in ways that build the capacity of individuals to contribute to the school's success.

- Leaders continuously strive to increase the degree to which everyone feels valued, respected, and appreciated. Leaders collect information, formally and informally, that helps them know how to improve relational issues. They identify and resolve issues promptly and professionally. They evidence great integrity and sincerity.

Source: Adapted from National Center for Urban School Transformation, 2011

A Resource or a Risk?

We know culture exists. We know it matters to our school improvement efforts. We know it needs to be nurtured and tended. Russell Hobby of Hay Group Education (2004) says of culture, "Used loosely the term can mean almost anything and loses utility as a tool for school improvement. Which is a shame, because school culture is the ultimate ceiling on our ability to transform our school and raise standards. Other initiatives, whether focusing on teaching strategies, leadership development, structure, teamwork, or collaboration, are wasted; doomed to deliver a fraction of their potential, without the right cultural supports. Viewed more positively, culture can also be the ultimate form of 'capacity'—a reservoir of energy and wisdom to sustain motivation and cooperation, shape relationships and aspirations, and guide effective choices at every level of the school."

Throughout this chapter we have discovered, with the help of many practicing educators, rigorous standards for school culture, and esteemed researchers, that a school's culture or climate can be a resource for school improvement or a risk to the implementation of even the best-laid strategic plans. The culture and climate of a school can be negatively affected by many factors: from major disciplinary problems such as bullying and violence to minor classroom rowdiness; from educator cynicism and hopelessness to student apathy and disengagement. It can also be positively influenced by everyone's conviction and commitment to high expectations, a profound belief that all can learn given the support of time and opportunity, and a pervasive insistence that both students and adults deserve respectful and compassionate care. Research shows quite clearly that schools perceived as being positive, safe, and nurturing environments focused on student learning do better than schools that lack this positive climate.

So what does this business of culture and climate have to do with school leadership? Reforming and re-creating are signs of our times in education. Without a deliberate focus on engaging the promise and commitment of all stakeholders to work on this school improvement process, we will meet with more lackluster and failed attempts to generate and sustain efforts to improve teaching and learning. Beliefs and actions are fundamental to our ability to challenge and change what does not work. It is the ultimate form of capacity building. And isn't that the definition of teaching and learning, and our primary responsibility as school leaders?

Key Ideas

- Culture is the system of beliefs, values, and thoughts that are shared by a group that constitutes the norm for how individuals behave toward each other and approach their life and their work.
- Healthy school climates and cultures are necessary for people and practices to grow and flourish.

- Descriptors of culture and climate can be elusive and abstract unless they are connected to concrete and specific expectations for action.
- One of the primary and ultimate responsibilities of school leaders is to foster and sustain a healthy and productive school culture that is conducive to high levels of learning for both students and adults.
- Healthy cultures encourage dialogue and debate that is necessary for challenging the status quo.

Questions to Continue This Discussion

- Have you considered assessing your current school culture with a survey or other measurement tool that defines strengths and areas of need about the way people treat each other in your learning community?
- How do school leaders ensure that even the smallest aspect of daily school life aligns with the core beliefs, values, and vision of the school?
- How do the rigor and coherence of curricular programs contribute to a positive school culture?
- How does monitoring the effect data of student achievement and the cause data of adult actions impact the instructional program and ultimately the school culture?

CHAPTER FOUR

The Resourceful Leader: Managing a Learning System

"The secret to getting ahead is getting started. The secret of getting started is breaking down your complex overwhelming tasks into small manageable tasks, and then starting on the first one."

MARK TWAIN

If you sat across the figurative aisle from my colleagues and me years ago learning about the historic and requisite skills and knowledge to become a licensed school administrator, you can possibly recall conversations about Kurt Lewin and authoritarian, democratic, and laissez-faire organizational management styles, transactional and transformational leadership attributes, and other abstract and theoretical distinctions between managing and leading. However, it is not until the opportunity to actually lead a school community appears on our professional doorstep that we begin to apply some of those conceptual aspects of textbook learning. It is then that we fully appreciate that the black and white, either/or, right or wrong propositions we discussed in those classes no longer seem so absolute or conclusive.

We are a bit dazed and confused to say the least by the arbitrary nature of many parts of our work in a learning system.

Your educational training was probably similar to mine, and perhaps you were taught to focus more on leadership skills and less on management skills. At the time of my preparation, the belief was that leaders had followers, which was good, and managers had subordinates, which was bad. Leaders wanted change, which was good, and managers desired stability and the status quo, which was bad. Leaders motivated, which was good, and managers rewarded, which was bad. Leaders liked visions, which was good, and managers liked plans, which was bad. Leading involved the soft skills of inspiration and enthusiasm; managing involved the hard skills of creating organizational charts and operational budgets. You get the picture. Management skills were sometimes diminished and discarded as an ineffective way to accomplish the complex responsibilities in schools. But as is often the case when ideas are applied to real life, "and" is a better conjunction than "or" for describing the work of school leaders. Leadership and management are both necessary functions to promote quality teaching and learning and the success of every student. One without the other advances an incomplete and inaccurate view of the tasks of school leadership.

My experiences with leadership as a watchful spectator and engaged participant have crystallized my thinking about managing and leading. I appreciate the advice that Stephen Covey shared in his helpful resource, *Principle-Centered Leadership* (1990). He divided the roles people play in organizations into three responsibilities—producers, managers, and leaders—and he advocated that all three were critical to the observed and documented success of an enterprise. Producers implemented—no work got done without them. Managers ensured that the producers were doing the work within a coherent structure and system, accomplishing it with speed, efficiency, and quality. Leaders ensured that the focus was on the right work, and leaders provided the direction, inspiration, and motivation to act in accordance with the shared vision and mission. These very concrete distinctions helped me understand that attention to all three functions in an organization contributes to achieving its collective goals.

Covey warns us that if there is not strong leadership present, the work can potentially be accomplished quickly and adeptly, but it might ultimately be the wrong work. As a result, the effort expended does not foster continued improvement and progress toward the aligned purpose of the system. He described this phenomenon as placing the ladder on the wrong wall. We can successfully reach the top rung only to discover that the climb does not guarantee that we have moved any closer to our desired outcome. Other business experts on managerial and leadership work such as Warren Bennis (1994), John Kotter (1996), Peter Senge (2006), Peter Drucker (1990), W. Edwards Deming (2000), and Tom Peters (2010), just to name a few, indicate that there are subtle differences between leadership and management, but all agree that both are necessary for accomplishing complex and challenging work.

The Ends and the Means

I tend to chunk my learning into digestible pieces, and what is most useful to me are the learnings that somewhat match my personal and professional experiences. Another way to represent this is that for new information to be valuable, the ends or goals must connect logically to the means or processes. With almost a half century of commitment to education in some capacity, I hold some very strong beliefs and assumptions about what is essential for reaching that end result of teaching and learning excellence, and I am not shy about sharing my ideas about effecting the means to get there. This chapter is a forum for stating my case.

Leadership, for me, is about people, and management is about the practices, policies, and procedures that the people engage in to successfully accomplish a task. Leadership is creative and relational, and management is directive and functional. Management works through a formal hierarchy of organizational control, and leadership relies on local influence and shared power. My deeply held belief, strengthened by extensive reading and reflection and diverse leadership experiences, is that people are not managed; they volunteer to be led. Time is managed, systems are managed, resources are managed, and environments are managed, but people choose to follow an idea or a mission they think will make a vital difference in the world. Exhibit 4.1 illustrates some of the basic distinctions between the two approaches.

EXHIBIT 4.1 Defining Management and Leadership

Management is a **process** for:	**Leadership** is a **relationship** for:
• Planning • Budgeting • Supervising • Evaluating	• Selecting talent • Inspiring • Coaching • Building trust

Leadership *or* Management

School leaders who have not developed their management skills or don't attend to them regularly set a direction or vision that others are to follow without giving much consideration to how the new direction is going to be achieved. Other people then have to work hard to "put meat on the bones of the dream." Leaders who are not effective managers see big-picture ideas but do not attach the necessary strategic planning steps or apply the principles of organizational management to align and integrate the multiple subsystems that are required for implementation with fidelity. The absence of good managerial skills can denote the difference between the success and failure of a project or initiative that ultimately defines the success or failure of the entire vision or mission of the learning system. As a result of this obvious gap, school leaders who are not effective managers can be very frustrating to work with. The producers who are responsible for accomplishing the objective become disillusioned and discouraged if they are asked to do something that lacks clarity or definition, or is short on indicators for success.

On the other hand, school managers who are less comfortable as leaders tend to control the resources to maintain the status quo or ensure that things happen according to established plans with limited thought devoted to a desired outcome or shared future. Management's focus is on solutions and avoiding organizational chaos and risk by systematically putting things in order. School managers do this by developing a plan with an accompanying budget that attempts to align with the goals of the institution but sometimes is restrictive and closed to innovation. This plan is usually short term and handles anything having to do with the day-to-day operations of the system. To support the implementation of the plan, managers create an organizational structure or hierarchy. These are necessary functions, but their ultimate goal should be to support leadership decisions that guide the way.

Leadership *and* Management

Peter Northouse, along with many others, advocates a combination of authentic leadership and management skills to ensure that systems provide and preserve safe, efficient, and effective environments for learning. He outlines how this can be accomplished (see Exhibit 4.2) in his widely read text on school administration, *Leadership: Theory and Practice* (2007).

EXHIBIT 4.2 Northouse's Alignment of Management and Leadership

Management Produces Order and Consistency	Leadership Produces Change and Movement
• Planning and budgeting • Establishing agendas • Setting timetables • Allocating resources	• Establishing direction • Creating a vision • Clarifying the big picture • Setting strategies
• Organizing and staffing • Providing structure • Making job placements • Establishing rules and procedures	• Aligning people • Communicating goals • Seeking commitment • Building teams, networks, and coalitions
• Controlling and problem solving • Developing incentives • Generating creative solutions • Taking corrective action	• Motivating and inspiring people • Energizing and empowering individuals • Satisfying unmet needs

Source: Adapted from Northouse, 2007, p. 10

Terrence Deal and Kent Peterson (1999) caution us to rethink our tendency to adopt a dualistic approach to leadership and management, and to avoid focusing on the opposing parts rather than the unifying concepts. The probability that school and district administrators need to be both leader and manager, to create both meaning and order, to both support change and defend the status quo, and to balance tradition with innovation is real. Principals and teacher leaders face dilemmas in schools every day that require expertise in leading all kinds of people and managing all kinds of processes, from simple to complicated.

Schools and classrooms need efficient functions and energizing relationships focused on a shared and attainable vision of the future. A learning system—whether it be an entire school or an individual classroom—that is over-managed and under-led results in unmotivated, disengaged, and underperforming children and adults. The Goldilocks factor of finding just the right balance between leading and managing in both contexts is paramount to successful teaching and learning.

More than ever before, in today's climate of heightened expectations and increased accountability, principals are obliged to improve teaching and learning. We are required to be educational visionaries, instructional and curriculum leaders, assessment experts, disciplinarians, community builders, public relations spokespersons, budget analysts, facility managers, special programs administrators, and responsive overseers of legal, contractual, and policy mandates and initiatives. We are expected to mediate the often-conflicting interests of parents, teachers, students, district office officials, unions, and state and federal agencies, and we also need to be sensitive to the increasingly diverse needs of students. This sounds like a challenging responsibility and probably explains why there is a shortage of educators standing in line for the opportunity to accept all of these leadership and management expectations. The good news is that there are thousands and thousands of illustrations across the country that indicate these tasks can be successfully and thoughtfully accomplished, with students being the ultimate beneficiaries.

Total Quality Management

In the early 1990s, Total Quality Management (TQM) was finding its way into schools. There seemed to be a natural and uncontrived fit between the principles and practices of producing quality goods and services and promoting excellence in education. The concepts formulated by founder W. Edwards Deming were based upon the assumption that people wanted to consistently display their best attitudes and present their best efforts in any endeavor, and it was a leader's job to enable them to do so by constantly assessing the system in which they worked for alignment and utility. That belief was certainly no stranger to teaching and learning. The requirements of teamwork, training, and the extensive collection and analysis of data to inform decision making made as much sense to our work in schools as it did on the assembly line.

At the time, my district was very invested in learning more about how continuous quality improvement and the application of some of these key principles could benefit our efforts in educational planning and reform. I was fortunate to have the opportunity to investigate and study specifically how this model could guide and support the intricate and challenging work of opening a new school. After some robust debates about who our customer was, how learning and curriculum fit into the terminology of quality, and what our product was, we got down to the business at hand and discovered some salient points of agreement between the TQM movement and our district reform initiatives. Some of these relationships were germane to me:

- Quality is not applied; it is developed.
- Learn together. Teamwork and collaboration are essential for improving the performance and production of the entire group.
- Words like command, control, competition, and compliance

are replaced with community, coherence, communication, and character.

- Self-evaluation, not supervision, is key to continuous improvement, where demonstrated models of talent and strength are respected and the benefits of visible learning are rewarded.
- Assessment data collected and analyzed along the way are more effective in quality management than assessment data collected and analyzed at the end.
- Systems and processes support people; they fail before the people do.
- All organizations are learning systems where research- and practice-based information guides decisions about policies and procedures.
- Leadership must be shared.
- Accountability for the success of the mission is accepted as everyone's responsibility.
- Exemplars of success and intelligent risk taking must be celebrated.

These 10 TQM implications became standards for our planning work at Elementary 25. They provided authentic measurements for how we were progressing with the leadership and management requirements of opening a new school and are certainly evident in the *ISLLC 2008* policy standards.

Educational Leadership Policy Standards: ISLLC 2008

School administrators create and manage an environment that is conducive to our core work of teaching and learning. *ISLLC 2008* Standard 3 addresses the need to build and sustain an organization that has coherent structures in place and access to adequate resources to guarantee students are learning at high levels. The implied balance of leadership and management expectations is evident in this standard.

> **Standard 3:** An education leader promotes the success of every student by ensuring management of the organization, operation, and resources for a safe, efficient, and effective learning environment.
>
> **Functions:**
> - Monitor and evaluate the management and operational systems.
> - Obtain, allocate, align, and efficiently utilize human, fiscal, and technological resources.
> - Promote and protect the welfare and safety of students and staff.
> - Develop the capacity for distributed leadership.
> - Ensure teacher and organizational time is focused to support quality instruction and student learning.
>
> Source: Council of Chief State School Officers, 2008

This standard sounds a bit repetitive after our lengthy discussion about school leadership and management, doesn't it? The benefits of Standard 3 and its functions are tangible, measurable, and directly connect to the tenets of Total Quality Management. As a result of demonstrated fidelity to this standard, people feel competent and confident about their work with students. They take greater pride in and ownership of their profession. Relationships among staff members at the school are more honest, open, and collaborative. Administrators feel less isolated and pressured as the burdens of leadership are shared. Successes increase and quality becomes the norm as instructional processes are improved continuously. With organizational change comes the opportunity for personal and professional growth, along with the rewards and satisfaction that come with getting better and better every day, and helping others do the same.

Although the philosophy of Total Quality Management originated from the world of business, it transcends the narrow commercial imperatives of increased productivity and profitability. TQM, at its heart, is dedicated to bringing out the best qualities in ourselves, in others, and in the work we do together. It is, in many ways, a natural fit with the hopes and aspirations of educational leaders in their work to improve schools and learning communities, and is a logical support to the successful implementation of *ISLLC 2008* Standard 3.

Another useful tool that assists school leaders in determining how to align the fiscal, human, and material resources to support the learning of all students is the Implementation Audit™ developed by The Leadership and Learning Center. Its purpose is to prioritize the school or district initiatives that are being implemented with fidelity and that have a direct, significant, and evidence-based positive effect on student achievement results. Districts across the nation are seeking a logical and publicly defensible approach to addressing the prevalent dilemma of diminished educational resources and the impact these potential budget cuts have on a comprehensive instructional program. In an effort to gain a deeper understanding of the level of implementation of priority initiatives and their impact on adult behaviors in the classroom and the resultant student academic performance, these audits provide valuable information through an extensive review of multiple sources of data about the levels of implementation.

The Implementation Audit™ process considers three essential questions to support the focus of *ISLLC 2008* Standard 3. First, what initiatives are currently in place and which initiatives are considered priorities? Second, what is the range of implementation for each of the prioritized initiatives? Third, what is the direct relationship between each prioritized initiative and improved student achievement? The purpose of the study is to provide useful information for teachers, administrators, and policymakers in making data-driven decisions, identifying and enhancing their strengths, and directly confronting their greatest academic challenges.

Elementary 25

Now to the real story of applying both the leadership and the management complexities that the planning team and I faced to create Elementary 25 as a benchmark school. From my vantage point as planning principal, I quickly realized that my responsibility included much more than sharing a vision of an exciting learning environment for students and adults and enthusiastically inviting others into the mix of school community members to engage and participate in the dream. That aspect of leadership was certainly critical, but the considerations for actually delivering on the promises implied that my routine and operational responsibilities were significant as well. We soon discovered that as stimulating and ethereal as our discussions about mission, vision, values, and beliefs were, they needed to be attached to more mundane and realistic decisions about what type of classroom furniture was desirable, what book titles were essential in the school library, how students would be assigned to teachers, how special schedules would be determined, and on and on. Discussions about how Elementary 25 would execute the tasks in the following list were as significant as the essential questions of who we were as educators and what we believed about teaching and learning. We discussed how to:

- incorporate consistent common planning time into the schedule for grade-level teachers to meet and collaborate.
- maximize instructional time and create longer learning blocks for literacy and math.
- organize teachers and students so that differentiation of curriculum, instruction, and assessment could be accomplished through special services and learning support teams.
- allocate and house instructional resources for equal access and effective use by teachers and students.
- ensure that school structures supported personal relationships between students and teachers.
- collect and analyze relevant data to monitor and formatively assess the instructional program and resultant student performance.
- address the physical and emotional welfare and safety issues of students and teachers to promote a healthy learning environment.
- determine and choose the most appropriate and aligned standards-based learning resources for literacy and math instruction.
- create a school-wide discipline approach that would be consistent and fair.
- allocate support for professional development that promotes the school's comprehensive curriculum design.
- invite new staff members to join the existing faculty and ensure their success with an induction program.
- integrate technology as a tool to enhance the instructional program.

- provide parents with information about how their children are doing academically and socially at school and include them as partners in the process.

All of these considerations became dynamic and lively conversations that we addressed as operational implications to support our vision of excellence for all.

One of the cautions we revisited over and over as a planning team was how our eagerness to collectively invent the best learning environment for students and adults could be translated into the necessary combination of design creativity and organizational coherence, or the "roots and wings" of the work. We did not want to think about possibilities and potential without providing the systems to ensure that the conditions for success were available. How could the developing platform for our educational focus result in concrete and credible policies and procedures that would guide our actions and be visible to our community? Which actions supported the strategic responsibilities for implementing long-term goals and which were essential for the day-to-day operational requirements that were more short term? How would these behaviors connect to our vision of building a community of learners, a positive climate for learning, a curriculum that would result in academic excellence, and a focus on character that would support constant displays of moral and ethical behavior? How could our symbols of a vision become substantive and not erode our enthusiasm and confidence that what we were planning could become a reality?

The team of 10 worked extensively exchanging apt and descriptive words, phrases, and ideas, and then the time came to add verbs to our plan and assign timetables and talent to the designated responsibilities. This proved to be one of the most challenging yet satisfying parts of the entire planning process. We were determining in stages that this work could be done and this dream could be realized. Teacher leaders emerged to present research-based practices for our consideration about a wide range of topics, including literacy and numeracy instruction, assessment tools, grouping patterns, professional learning options, parental involvement opportunities, resources and services for students, and school-wide discipline expectations. The synergy was palpable. We looked forward to our Tuesday meetings with a recognized anticipation close to prom night for teenagers or a wedding day for the bride and groom. The balance we achieved between leadership and management equated to the perfect blend of knowing and then doing.

What I did observe from that planning experience for Elementary 25 was how much good emerges when the principles and practices of a constant focus on quality take hold and become embedded in a school's culture. Excellence and quality become the watchwords in every aspect of school life. Tangible benefits for the adults and the students in the system were obvious. The excitement of action, the sense of pride, the strong relationships that were based upon trust, respect, and open and honest communication all contributed to an environment that was mediated by shared leadership implications and intentional management decisions. The entire team basked in the knowledge that they had accomplished an amazing feat that few professional educators could claim and no one could take away. Elementary 25 was on its way to becoming a beacon of hope and inspiration for teaching and learning innovation. Our vision was becoming intentional, thoughtful, and actionable through leadership and management decisions that were made collaboratively by that core team of 10

Key Ideas

- A complete and accurate picture of the work of a school principal includes both daring leadership ability and deliberate management skills.

- Management is necessary for producing order and consistency, and leadership is required to promote change and innovation.

- The challenge of school leadership to constantly improve teaching and learning forces us to balance the need to direct and the need to guide, the need to talk and the need to listen.

- Total Quality Management is a movement that has many connections to our work in education and can support our thinking and planning toward the goal of excellence for all of our students.

- The Leadership and Learning Center's Implementation Audit™ is a tool designed to support decisions in today's climate of increasingly diminished resources to determine which initiatives are implemented with fidelity and which contribute to improved student learning.

Questions to Continue This Discussion

- Have you had the opportunity to work with an individual with strong management skills but not very much capacity to lead? Describe the challenges of that experience.

- How does a strong manager differ from a strong leader?

- How does the concept of Total Quality Management fit with our goal to provide educational excellence and equity for all students?

- How would a tool like the Implementation Audit™ contribute to making data-driven decisions about which resources are supportive of increased student achievement?

CHAPTER FIVE

The Collaborative Leader: Partnering for the Benefit of Learning

> *"There is no such thing as a new idea. It is impossible. We simply take a lot of old ideas and put them into a sort of mental kaleidoscope. We give them a turn and they make new and curious combinations. We keep on turning and making new combinations indefinitely; but they are the same old pieces of colored glass that have been in use through all the ages."*
>
> MARK TWAIN

Smart school leaders are great collaborators. Out of necessity they foster a cultural expectation of shared and distributed leadership. They understand early on that when creating consistently successful teaching and learning opportunities, everyone needs to work together to accomplish the daunting challenge of educating all students to high levels. Mark Twain reminds us in this quote, however, that there are few new ideas, just new combinations of old ones. That certainly holds true in my experience. Rarely did I participate in a professional dialogue that presented some startling new research or surprising theoretical hypothesis; our conversations always involved rethinking an established belief or assumption about education with the refocused spotlight of inquiry and discovery on the topic. Those discussions and debates required many minds to offer new perspectives and new insights for consideration to validate the old ideas and connect them in a new system of approaches and strategies.

Examining how to invite and welcome all stakeholders into the sustained process of teaching and learning; how to promote respect for everyone's contributions and diverse opinions; how to instill enthusiasm for designing and delivering lessons that maximize student engagement and success; how to systematically assess how well we are doing and provide additional support and enrichment to those who need it; how to create a collaborative community of learners; and how to inspire the capacity and inclination to do more with less represents nothing novel in our work. These are critical functions of educational leadership that are prevalent and powerful responsibilities, and we must learn to execute them with competence, confidence, and commitment.

This realization is really good news and offers hope and optimism. It emphasizes the fact that teachers and principals collectively possess virtually all of the answers to the dilemmas we face in providing quality education for everyone. The key to move from advocacy to action is figuring out whom to partner with to effectively respond to the needs and interests of our unique learning communities. This chapter explores the potency of collaboration to achieve these goals of educational excellence and equity. Leaders never could do it alone, and now more than ever they need everyone's input and contribution to promote the success of every student.

Professional Learning Communities

Partnerships imply a shared accountability for improvement. They build common and agreed-upon knowledge by exploring perplexing questions and potential solutions that positively impact the students and adults in their learning system. The compelling and extensive work of Richard DuFour and company with professional learning communities (PLCs) illustrates that the combined engagement of many competent individuals creates and sustains communities of common focus and best practice, which ultimately supports student success.

DuFour defines collaboration as a systematic process in which people work together independently to analyze and impact professional practice in order to improve individual and collective results. In a PLC, collaboration focuses on the critical questions of learning:

- What is it we want each student to learn?
- How will we know when each student has learned it?
- How will we respond when a student experiences difficulty in learning?
- How will we enrich and extend the learning for students who are proficient?

DuFour's description of what a school that is a professional learning community looks like is:

- The daily work of the school is driven by common purpose, shared vision, and collective commitments.
- There are high expectations regarding student achievement and a commitment on the part of staff to accept responsibility for student learning.
- The learning of each student is monitored on a timely basis using common core curriculum and common assessments aligned with state standards.

- School structures support student learning and provide additional time and support for students who initially do not achieve intended outcomes.
- Job-embedded professional development leads to the collective identification of, reflection about, and implementation of best practices for improved student achievement.
- Staff members work collaboratively in processes that foster continuous improvement in all indicators of student achievement.
- The use of data promotes an action orientation and focus on results.
- Leadership of school improvement processes is widely dispersed and helps sustain a culture of continuous improvement.

Source: Adapted from DuFour, DuFour, and Eaker, 2008

DuFour's description sounds like a pretty comprehensive and thorough plan for collective accountability for student achievement. And again, there are no new or innovative ideas about the purpose of schooling or shortcuts on how to accomplish the work listed here, just solid and simple advice on how to redesign and reinvent a culture to become more collaborative for the benefit of improved teaching and learning. Another reason for optimism: we have a road map to guide our journey to that goal of improvement.

Can Collaboration Be Taught?

Robert Garmston asks this question in a 1997 article in the *Journal of Staff Development* and provides some noteworthy answers. His contention is that just as musicians and athletes practice fundamentals, so do people who want to master the art and science of collaboration. The basic skills of collaboration are communication, creating opportunities for advocacy and inquiry, resolving differences, solving problems, making decisions, and engaging in reflection. Educational communities must learn these skills to ensure their students benefit from adults working together in a spirit of respect and trust to support their success. There are both content and processes that need to be introduced, practiced, and coached so they become intentional, automatic, and the norm for the school culture.

Collaboration involves working with others to invent, create, build models, solve dilemmas, and produce effects. Adults and students learn more when they collaborate; they work harder, they support one another intellectually and emotionally, and they commit to cumulative and cooperative expectations, efforts, and results. It is an essential method of relating to one another and provides a structure for deep communication and improved performance. Bottom line, it is a more engaging and satisfying way to accomplish intricate and challenging assigned responsibilities.

Douglas Reeves (2004) states that collaboration is hard work and that genuine skillfulness in it is acquired over time through focused practice and reflection on important tasks. It represents much more than just getting along in the workplace and enjoying each other's company socially. It goes far beyond collegiality. His recommendation is to begin the vital work of studying exemplars of student work to determine a common definition of proficiency as an induction into the world of professional collaboration. In this culture of authentic experimentation and close examination, collaborative scoring of student work provides opportunities to work together in a productive capacity to reach consensus on something important. It grows the skills of purposeful collaboration and emphasizes the power of teams to achieve the goals of the learning system.

Most educational problems are too complex for simple or linear solutions. They require multiple perspectives to correctly assess the current situation, imagine a realistic answer, and develop and commit to a plan to achieve that solution. Collaboration moves us from isolation to integration and from advocacy to inquiry. The thinking process becomes a product of "us," not "you or me." Ideas are presented, elaborated upon and enhanced, and finally accepted as a group decision about what needs to be accomplished. Collaboration becomes an automatic and a fluent process that requires an awareness of our collective feelings, intentions, and influence. It promotes ownership of the work and provides motivation and commitment to successfully complete it.

People who feel empowered and, as a result, take ownership of decisions and promote a tremendous sense of pride in what they do characterize a successful learning organization. The climate that is established supports the vision and mission of teaching and learning. Collaboration fosters risk taking, rewards innovation, and distributes necessary information to everyone fairly and accurately. All of these components contribute to an environment that values trust, respect, and choice among students and adults alike, and the result is enhanced learning for all.

Getting Smarter Together

A colloquial definition of collaboration is getting smarter together. John Hattie (2009) in his seminal synthesis of over 800 meta-analyses relating to student achievement describes the conversations that teachers and principals engage in as supporting one another's strengths and accommodating or mitigating their weaknesses. He advocates working together to increase the available pool of instructional ideas and resources. As a result of collaboration, schools become better prepared and systematically organized to examine and test new ideas, methods, and strategies that allow faculties to become more adaptable, self-reliant, and interdependent. Effective collaboration eases the challenge of retaining talented teachers, mentoring teachers new to the profession, and providing induction support to instill cultural norms, values, and traditions in both veteran and rookie staff members.

Supporting Hattie's research in education is Liz Wiseman, author of *Multipliers: How the Best Leaders Make Everyone Smarter* (2010). She contends that in the business world organizations sometimes find smart, talented people and then promote them to leadership roles. But many of these people cling to their own capabilities and fail to appreciate, utilize, and develop the full genius of their team. They may be smart individual leaders, but they shut down the smarts of others and have a draining or diminishing impact on their performance. These "diminishers" come at a high cost to the system because they waste the talent and the intellect of team members, get less than half of the capability of the people around them, and reduce the intelligence and capacity of their organizations at a time when we currently need leaders who can do much more with fewer resources.

In contrast, Wiseman calls the best leaders "multipliers," and describes them as:

- talent magnets who attract and optimize talent.
- liberators who create intensity that requires best thinking.
- challengers who extend challenges.
- debate makers who debate before deciding.
- investors who instill ownership and accountability.

When leaders use their intelligence to amplify the intelligence and capabilities of people around them, they inspire employees to stretch themselves to deliver results that surpass everyone's expectations.

These leaders who are multipliers hold a distinct set of assumptions about intelligence. Whereas diminishers see a limited number of smart people and assume that no one else will figure things out without leadership, multipliers see an abundance of intelligent people and assume that people are smart enough to solve the problems on their own.

The core assumptions of this book recognize that leaders who are multipliers see genius in others, create intensity that requires best thinking, extend challenges, debate decisions, and finally inspire ownership and accountability for those decisions. Imagine what would be possible in our schools and classrooms if everyone had this mindset and believed that we could double the potential of the people around us, in both student and adult performance. Wiseman suggests that if we shift from giving answers to asking insightful and challenging questions that cause us to stop, think, and reflect, we will multiply the results. If we as leaders dispense our ideas in small incremental doses and invite the brilliance of others to shine through, rather than flooding the room with our brilliance, the contributions of the group will be magnified. If we encourage and allow people to take risks by trying innovative ideas rather than just pointing out problems without solutions, the productive engagement of people would increase exponentially.

In education, intelligence through collaboration might be our most underutilized asset. And isn't that a sad commentary on how we currently approach our work?

In order to intentionally get smarter together in schools, we must deliberately spend team time learning what works best to effect positive learning results for students. Through collaboration and inquiry, all viewpoints and voices are heard to inform what we do, why and how we do it, and, in the final analysis, how well we do it. The process of building shared professional knowledge by answering these questions requires that we investigate research-based practices regarding teaching and learning and infuse them into the current context of our school or district. The Data Teams process helps immeasurably with this endeavor.

Data Teams

Douglas Reeves (2010b) endorses the Data Teams process, created by The Leadership and Learning Center, as the single best way to assist educators in moving from "drowning in data" to using relevant information to make informed and collaborative decisions about instruction. The distinguishing factor that makes Data Teams unique is that student test scores are not the only indicator of success or failure, but the combination of student results, teaching strategies, and leadership support is considered together to make that determination. "Data Teams give professionals respect, reinforcement, and feedback—the keys for improved impact on student learning" (Reeves, 2010ba).

The Data Teams process is designed to be both a collaborative tool to assist in data-driven decision making for improved student learning and an authentic professional development opportunity for improved adult learning. Exhibit 5.1 illustrates each step in the process.

The collaborative structures of the Data Teams process support acceleration and remediation for learners through a transparent and honest look at student data, a review of best instructional practices, and an accounting of leadership actions to determine the effects of our work on cohorts of students. The learning that is explored through this cycle is not limited to just students. Adults also benefit by participating in powerful professional development experiences with their colleagues through discussions about effective instructional strategies, formative assessment results, and indicators of success.

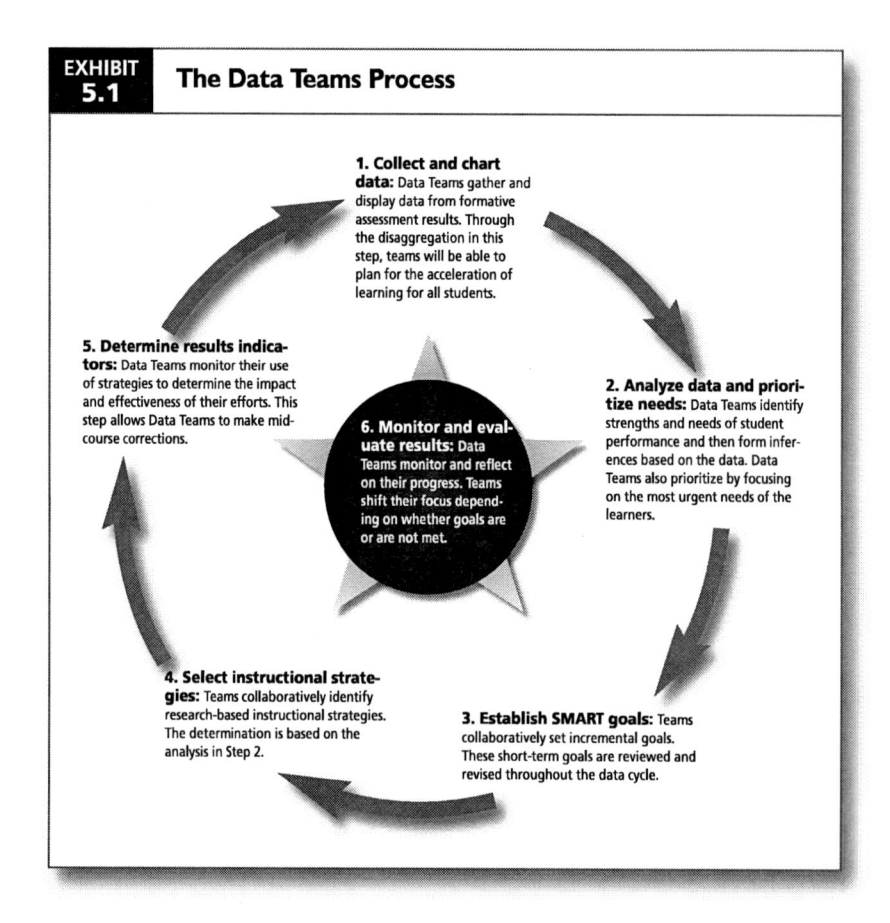

EXHIBIT 5.1 The Data Teams Process

1. Collect and chart data: Data Teams gather and display data from formative assessment results. Through the disaggregation in this step, teams will be able to plan for the acceleration of learning for all students.

2. Analyze data and prioritize needs: Data Teams identify strengths and needs of student performance and then form inferences based on the data. Data Teams also prioritize by focusing on the most urgent needs of the learners.

3. Establish SMART goals: Teams collaboratively set incremental goals. These short-term goals are reviewed and revised throughout the data cycle.

4. Select instructional strategies: Teams collaboratively identify research-based instructional strategies. The determination is based on the analysis in Step 2.

5. Determine results indicators: Data Teams monitor their use of strategies to determine the impact and effectiveness of their efforts. This step allows Data Teams to make mid-course corrections.

6. Monitor and evaluate results: Data Teams monitor and reflect on their progress. Teams shift their focus depending on whether goals are or are not met.

Leaders Make It Happen!: An Administrator's Guide to Data Teams by Brian McNulty and Laura Besser (2011) emphasizes that the big ideas for helping us effectively use data to improve learning are the following:

- Teachers and leaders matter in terms of the outcomes that students are getting.
- It is what teachers and leaders do that matters the most.
- Schools and districts get better outcomes when they focus and learn from that focus.
- The primary focus should be on instruction.

- Implementation, monitoring, feedback, and support all matter.
- Data should provide a starting point and focus actions, help assess progress, and identify where methods are successful and where there is a need for more support.
- Schools and districts, acting in alignment as a system, make improvements through data-driven inquiry and continuous learning.
- Teams help us inquire and learn more deeply, provide more effective guidance in terms of support, and provide opportunities for developing leadership, ownership, and accountability across the district.

To confirm these key assumptions, Covey (2004) reminds us that "people who have made a commitment to continual learning, growth, and improvement are those who have the ability to change, adapt, and flex with the changing realities of life." That statement represents our relentless pursuit of an agenda of continuous progress and our priority of learning as individuals and teammates, and makes the Data Teams process all the more relevant and authentic.

Motivation Theory

There has been much research done on motivation theory. For centuries we have tried to figure out what motivates people to accomplish extraordinary work. Daniel Pink in his book *Drive: The Surprising Truth about What Motivates Us* (2009) analyzes what engages us, what inspires us, and what influences us. His burning question is, "How do we think about what we do?" He states that if the work is purposeful, interesting, and self-directed, people do not need extrinsic motivation to successfully complete it. After basic needs are met, rewards actually get in the way of high performance on creative and complex tasks.

Pink's discussion about why we do what we do revolves around three concepts: autonomy, mastery, and purpose. We do what we do because we want control over our lives, we want to become progressively better and better at something that matters, and we want to be in the service of something that is larger than ourselves and benefits the greater good. We do not need carrots or sticks to engage more actively or perform more productively. What we do need, however, is an interesting task, flexible time to complete it, techniques that utilize our talents and skills, and the right team to work on the task together.

Mindset is an uncomplicated yet profound idea that will help us confirm some of the important ideas that Daniel Pink raises. World-renowned Stanford University psychologist Carol Dweck (2008), after decades of research on achievement and motivation, identifies two mindsets that play important roles in people's success. In one, the fixed mindset, people believe that talents and abilities are fixed traits. They think we inherit a certain amount of intelligence, and nothing can be done to change our allotted quota. Many years of research have now shown that when people adopt the fixed mindset, it can limit their perception of who they are as learners and what they can accomplish. They become overly concerned with publicly proving their talents and abilities and hiding their deficiencies and setbacks. Struggle and mistakes imply a predetermined lack of talent or ability. People with this mindset will actually pass up important opportunities to learn and grow if there is a risk of unmasking weaknesses.

In the other mindset, the growth mindset, people believe that their talents and abilities can be developed through passion, learning, and persistence. For them, it is not about looking smart or grooming their image of intelligence. It is a commitment to getting better at something, to applying effective and focused effort, and to taking informed risks and benefiting from honest feedback to improve the results. In a growth mindset, people create a love of learning and a resilience that is essential for great accomplishments. Virtually all successful people have the growth mindset because it instills motivation, honors hard work, and rewards a positive attitude.

Dweck (2008) concludes that we need to foster in any learner, adult or student, a mindset of accomplishment that is attached to effective effort, not inherent ability. We should encourage learners to stretch their potential and not limit natural eagerness or curiosity for discovery to preconceived notions of intelligence.

The power of fostering the growth mindset in our schools is dramatic for both students and adults. Some of our brightest students and most talented teachers avoid challenges. They are uncomfortable with showing that effort is necessary to accomplish a goal, and they wilt in the face of adversity because they are afraid of failing in front of their peers. In contrast, I have known resilient go-getters, who persist and achieve far more than anticipated when they work hard, request feedback, try again, and face obstacles head-on. If we establish and nurture a collaborative learning community and culture that promotes risk taking, supports inquiry, and rewards perseverance in learners, old and young, we are ready to confront any learning challenge. Learning how to learn and learning how to teach require the same diligence and focus, and the same attitudes of bravery and efficacy. Without a growth mindset, we will not move very far down the road of improved education.

These discoveries about motivation have powerful implications for leading, for teaching, and for learning. First, we do not have to try so hard at finding the right reward or incentive to motivate our performance. Rewards and incentives don't help. Second, educators who experience autonomy, mastery, and purpose complete the work with expertise and energy. We deeply learn what we deeply care about. And third, the results sharpen our thinking and accelerate our creativity, all good things that contribute to excellence. The motivation to collaborate is intrinsic in all of us.

Educational Leadership Policy Standards: ISLLC 2008

As school leaders, we are visible representatives to the broader community of the diverse values and beliefs that are present in our schools. How we advocate for the success of all of our students and how we use our community as a resource to accomplish the challenging goals and aspirations of our learning organization are critical to our success as school leaders. Equally important is how we partner and collaborate with individuals and groups to communicate and establish the necessary partnerships between the site and the larger community needs and interests. Standard 4 of the *ISLLC 2008* policy standards indicates the importance of engaging and leveraging community services that promote our success with all students.

> **Standard 4:** An education leader promotes the success of every student by collaborating with faculty and community members, responding to diverse community interests and needs, and mobilizing community resources.
>
> ### Functions:
> - Collect and analyze data and information pertinent to the educational environment.
> - Promote understanding, appreciation, and use of the community's diverse cultural, social, and intellectual resources.

> - Build and sustain positive relationships with families and caregivers.
> - Build and sustain productive relationships with community partners.
>
> Source: Council of Chief State School Officers, 2008

Exemplifying this standard requires that school leaders develop and demonstrate a set of highly refined skills that elicit and honor the multiple perspectives of the families and community members they serve. Actively engaging all stakeholders by communicating the planning, implementation, and evaluation strategies for accomplishing high levels of learning and requesting input and opinions about these goals are the essential leadership practices of collaboration and partnership. Becoming aware of the implications of this standard for effective leadership behaviors to promote shared investment in the success of all students is imperative to acknowledging communities as the vital resource for our work.

Elementary 25

The planning team at Elementary 25 had a unique and coveted opportunity to elevate collaboration to a new level in our work. We were able to establish a positive and productive learning community and culture for our students, families, and the broader community. Our team was motivated by our challenge to create the best learning environment possible, discover the best curriculum and instructional strategies available, investigate the best processes and practices to implement our plans, and, most important, invite the best people to join our staff. There certainly were no carrots or sticks necessary to move our ideas forward. This deeply rewarding project met all of the criteria for the desired commitment and required investment of intense collaboration and intrinsic motivation.

Building a school and becoming a learning community automatically and urgently engaged us in a creative, purposeful, and intellectually challenging endeavor. We were obliged by the sheer enormity of the responsibility to unleash all of the talent and capacity on the team to fulfill the many strategic and operational tasks inherent in designing, defining, and developing a dynamic community for learning. Our shared charge was to guarantee that every student was a confident, competent, and resourceful learner. This responsibility required every adult to become a multiplier—someone who saw the genius in everyone to engage in the best thinking and debate alternatives to the tried and sometimes tired approaches and actions of teaching and leading. We wanted to be inventive yet practical, directing our own destiny as a school community by researching and discovering what supported our beliefs and values and what would result in a comprehensive, coherent, yet compellingly compassionate environment for enriching learning opportunities and experiences for everyone.

What transpired was exactly what was described in this chapter. Dedicated and wise people who owned the outcome of creating a place that represented a shared vision of learning collaborated at a very high level to encounter and undertake bold ideas to foster what was necessary to reach that vision. Our sophisticated understanding of what it would take to accomplish this huge professional and personal challenge aligned us. This ownership of ideas specified that everyone was willing to be in the same boat at the same time, and the alignment of actions stipulated that we all needed to energetically row in the same direction to move upstream. No external rewards were necessary. The work itself was autonomous, masterful, and purposeful.

What resulted from this amazing collaborative effort was a

tremendously successful school, filled with eager students, enthusiastic adults, and a high-performing culture that promoted and expected excellence in every aspect of our day. Many of my colleagues asked what types of team-building activities were generated to establish trusting and respectful relationships and what other tools were necessary to collaborate at this level. They were surprised to hear that the difficulty and significance of the work built the teams. We did not engage in the traditional ropes course, trust fall, or other disclosures of faith in each other's ability or commitment. The intensity of the work, the ownership of the process, and the commitment to the outcome were enough to cement us as a team and build the requisite accountability for results. It was a rare, sometimes fragile, yet incredibly resilient relationship and one that was nurtured and sustained through many tests and trials. It was the true exemplar of collaboration.

Key Ideas

- Teachers and principals collectively possess the solutions to the dilemmas that plague us in improving education.
- Professional learning communities imply a shared and committed accountability for educational improvement.
- The purpose of collaboration is to gain multiple perspectives through inquiry and integration of different ideas and experiences.
- Multipliers amplify the intelligence and capacity of people and have the potential of doubling their performance on a challenging task.
- Extrinsic rewards and incentives are not necessary when the work is creative, purposeful, and self-directing.
- The Data Teams process is an effective collaborative tool that

supports student achievement and adult professional learning.

Questions to Continue This Discussion

- Do you agree with Mark Twain that there are no new ideas, just new combinations of old ones? Why or why not?
- What does collaborative leadership look like, sound like, and feel like to a team?
- Can collaboration be taught, and, if so, what are some of the necessary skills, competencies, and capacities needed to do it well?
- How can the concepts of professional learning communities and Data Teams be integrated to promote collaboration among colleagues?
- Describe a situation when you experienced the impact of having interesting and important work on your intrinsic motivation to accomplish that work.

CHAPTER SIX

The Ethical Leader: Leading with Integrity

"It is curious that physical courage should be so common in the world and moral courage so rare."

"If you tell the truth, you don't have to remember anything."

MARK TWAIN

Our words and deeds are what make us undeniably human. They represent who we are as people, our values, our beliefs—the "shoulds" and the "oughts" of our lives. In the early to mid-1800s, Horace Mann, the father of the common school, acknowledged that public schools should help students develop both reason and conscience. The *Common School Journal*, which Mann edited, stated, "The highest and noblest office of education pertains to our moral nature." This statement has as much relevance and meaning currently as it did more than a century and a half ago. Today's schools need to recommit to this responsibility of teaching virtue before knowledge, or at least alongside it, to ensure that our world not only survives as a kinder and gentler place but also thrives as one. In order to do this, we as school leaders must stand up and be counted for what is true and right and fill that sometimes awkward silence that appears when we begin to talk about moral and ethical standards in education.

Honesty, respect, trustworthiness, fairness, compassion, perseverance, giving, responsibility, self-discipline, and citizenship are words that have power for everyone. These ideas, combined with deliberate and congruent actions, add invincible dimension to who we are as adults, what we model, and who our students can become. We are finally recovering the wisdom of Horace Mann that we do share a basic morality that affirms our human dignity, provides for the welfare of one person as well as for the common good of many, and does not infringe on our rights and freedoms as individuals. Adults promote this morality by teaching directly and indirectly the values that transcend cultures, religions, and other orientations and beliefs. What our students learn from us touches their deepest selves and helps them become not only more knowledgeable but also more socially and ethically responsible. What is learned in school in combination with the home is imperative to answering life's most important questions.

Schools have an obligation to provide leadership for social justice issues, assure systemic equity, and provide democratic treatment for everyone. I argue that this is not merely a subjective preference for how to meet a leadership standard but has substantive worth for our entire society and our collective conscience. The best school leaders draw on these moral qualities to influence others through inspiration, modeling, and trusting relationships. They do the courageous things despite high costs and risks, and they do them not because they will yield approval or advantage, but because it is the right and just response for their learning community. Ethical school leaders strive to meet the classical tests of "reversibility" (Would you want to be treated this way?) and "universalizability" (Would you want all persons to act this way in a similar situation?) (Lickona, 1993).

The Resurgence of Character Education in Our Schools

The Basic School: A Community for Learning, written by Ernest Boyer in 1995, advocated for a foundationally sound education institution. In his plan, after creating community, developing a curriculum with coherence, and fostering a climate for learning, came committing to character. His bold words inspired many school leaders across the nation to quit apologizing for our belief that schools helped shape the ethical and moral lives of our children. We took his endorsement as permission to follow our hearts and minds and reengage in dialogues about excellence in living as well as learning.

Today there are an increasing number of educators who believe our nation is more deeply in moral trouble than in the 1990s. Increased signs of the breakdown of the family unit, examples of the lack of respect and civility in everyday life, media that portrays violence, materialism, and promiscuity as societal norms, just to name a few examples, all point to the need for school leaders to move from being ethical bystanders to being advocates for and models of integrity, fairness, and equity in word and deed. Our leadership obligation is to help everyone, young and old, become a smart and good person. To accomplish this we must:

- foster a compassionate and caring attitude beyond our classrooms to inspire generosity, giving, and service to our greater community.

- amplify the school-wide culture to the highest moral ground to consistently honor respect, responsibility, perseverance, citizenship, and honesty as the nonnegotiable code of conduct and moral compass for everyone.

- model principles of fairness, integrity, respect for diversity, and trustworthiness so that all who are involved with teaching and learning feel valued and respected for who they are and what they can contribute.

- partner with parents, faith-based organizations, local businesses, and government agencies to promote the core characteristics of ethical behavior in our schools and communities.

- advocate for responsive and supportive treatment for members of our entire learning community.

The ancient Greek philosopher Heraclitus is credited with the saying, "Character is destiny." That certainly applies to both adults and students alike. As we face our deepest societal issues, we need to remember that the moral imperative we must attend to is ensuring that our schools work for all, are accountable to all, and provide for all.

Moral Imperatives: Beyond Compliance to Commitment

Michael Fullan (2001) defines moral purpose as, "Acting with the intention of making a positive difference in the lives of employees, customers, and society as a whole." He lists the commitment to moral purpose as an imperative for educational leaders to engage in personally, and, as a result, to mobilize and inspire others in the organization to act beyond compliance and be guided by the deliberate actions that matter to everyone.

The choice between what is right and what is wrong is a central issue in organizational decision making and hence in leadership. The underlying question is which values and whose values dictate this choice, but the desired outcome is the same and informs that choice: improving the quality of life for everyone as they live and work together. That involves raising the achievement and performance bar and closing the gap for the most disadvantaged of our nation's students. Fullan also argues that our moral imperative drives all of our authentic leadership work to change and reform our educational system. It fosters a focus on the outcome of increased achievement for all and gives coherence to any change initiative that is endorsed. This helps us define what is important and what is not and supports educators to decide what actions to take based upon those definitions.

Thomas Sergiovanni states in *The Lifeworld of Leadership: Creating Culture, Community and Personal Meaning in Our schools* (2000) that "authentic leaders anchor their practice in ideas, values, and commitments, exhibit distinctive qualities of style and substance, and can be trusted to be morally diligent in advancing the enterprises they lead. Authentic leaders, in other words, display character, and character is the defining characteristic of authentic leadership." Both thought leaders, Fullan and Sergiovanni, advise that moral purpose must be accompanied by leadership strategies that inspire people to actively work to improve the lives of their students and pursue the same goals of equity and excellence for all. And they conclude by saying that leaders must remember to make heroes of the people who deliver on this promise because of the depth of those heroes' commitment to making a positive difference in the world.

Educational Leadership Policy Standards: ISLLC 2008

ISLLC 2008 Standard 5 indicates that school leaders serve as models of the highest standards of professionalism at their site and in their communities. Their work is guided and informed by a set of universal moral and ethical principles. They inspire, encourage, and motivate others by demonstrating their constant commitment to teaching and learning and providing equal opportunity and access to quality in both. They develop and sustain this commitment through their own lifelong pursuit of professional learning and reflective practice.

> **Standard 5:** An education leader promotes the success of every student by acting with integrity, fairness, and in an ethical manner.
>
> **Functions:**
> - Ensure a system of accountability for every student's academic and social success.
> - Model principles of self-awareness, reflective practice, transparency, and ethical behavior.
> - Safeguard the values of democracy, equity, and diversity.
> - Consider and evaluate the potential moral and legal consequences of decision making.
> - Promote social justice and ensure that individual student needs inform all aspects of schooling.
>
> Source: Council of Chief State School Officers, 2008

Great school leaders have the moral purpose for schooling front and center as the basis and foundation for personal and professional ethics that place the needs and interests of students, families, staff, and the greater community ahead of everything else. They influence the school culture by infusing the values of fairness, justice, respect, service, and integrity among all adults. They assume responsibility for every student's success and use data to plan, implement, and evaluate the teaching and learning daily practices to refine and improve them.

Great decision makers utilize what I call the "three Rs of intelligent thought"—rehearsal, response, and reflection—to model the continuous pursuit of the primary purpose of improved teaching and learning in our schools. This type of leadership values ownership in collective inquiry and collaboration and the alignment of beliefs so that everyone is working toward the same desired outcome. Good decisions are made twice. First, good decisions are practiced; they are visualized or rehearsed in the mind before action is taken. They are based upon accurate and complete data and are aligned with the mission and vision of the organization. Think about an important meeting or presentation that is in your future. To prepare, you determine what you want to accomplish and plan and practice to meet that end. After considerable rehearsal to anticipate most of the potential unknowns, you move forward with a response. That response is weighed and measured for effectiveness. Finally, after the action or the decision has been implemented, it lives again as a reflection of what worked and what needed to be modified. Intelligent decisions are a result of rehearsing what could happen, discovering what did happen, and reflecting on what should happen next time to ensure success.

Great motivators inspire our thoughts and actions to increase the level of everyone's feelings of significance and competence and raise the bar of performance. Leaders who motivate positive attitude and focused and effective effort realize that exceeding expectations is easier than first thought. We surprise ourselves at what can be accomplished when we believe in each other and build everyone's capacity for good. Great leaders lead as servants of their learning communities.

Servant Leadership

The concept of leadership known as "servant leadership" was promoted by Robert Greenleaf in the 1970s. Since then, there have been endorsements for striving to be the best caretaker, the best guardian, and the best keeper and protector you can be for those you lead from thought leaders such as Stephen Covey, M. Scott Peck, Peter Senge,

Peter Drucker, Ken Blanchard, Warren Bennis, Douglas Reeves, Peter Block, Margaret Wheatley, Thomas Sergiovanni, and James Kouzes and Barry Posner, to name a few. Servant leaders govern with integrity. This type of leadership evolves from an intrinsic and indelible set of core values and a deliberate choice of dedicated service over self-interest and self-advocacy.

Larry Spears (1996) offers 10 characteristics or qualities of servant leadership for our consideration:

- **Listening:** Servant leaders' communication skills are enhanced through a deep commitment to listening intently to the followers. Servant leaders seek to identify and clarify the will of the group. Receptive listening and reflection are essential to the growth of a servant leader.

- **Empathy:** Servant leaders strive to understand and empathize with others. They accept and recognize followers for their uniqueness; and they assume others have good intentions, even if they disagree with behavior or performance.

- **Healing:** Servant leaders are adept at healing others as well as themselves. They help make others whole by facilitating healing of attitudes or dispositions. Servant leaders share with followers the search for wholeness.

- **Awareness:** Servant leaders exhibit a general awareness of what is happening in the organization. They possess a keen sense of self-awareness and an understanding of issues involving ethics and values. Servant leaders are often described as disturbers and awakeners.

- **Persuasion:** Servant leaders employ persuasion rather than positional authority when making decisions within the organization. They prefer to convince rather than coerce followers. Servant leaders are very effective at building consensus within the group.

- **Conceptualization:** Servant leaders do not deal only with short-term goals and thinking. They are able to stretch their thinking to encompass broader-based conceptual thinking. Servant leaders can nurture the abilities of others to "dream great dreams" and to think beyond day-to-day realities.

- **Foresight:** Servant leaders are capable of understanding lessons from the past, seeing the realities of the present, and predicting likely consequences of decisions. They use intuitive thinking to help make the best decisions.

- **Stewardship:** Servant leaders are dedicated to holding their institutions in trust for the greater good of society. They are committed to serving the needs of others.

- **Commitment to the Growth of People:** Servant leaders believe in the intrinsic value of people beyond their tangible contributions as workers. They feel responsible for nurturing the personal, professional, and spiritual growth of employees.

- **Building Community:** Servant leaders are dedicated to rebuilding the sense of community that has been lost with the shift to large institutions.

Source: Adapted from Spears, 1996

Some believe that these characteristics represent a faith-based approach to leadership. I would argue that leading from a strong moral and ethical foundation requires these 10 qualities whether you follow an organized religion or not. Seeking the best in everyone, practicing good stewardship, and considering others first are practices of leadership with integrity and should be the focus of every great school leader. To quote Ben Franklin, "The noblest question in the world is,

'What good may I do in it?'" That statement appeals to and affirms the values that brought us into this service-oriented, mission-driven profession in the first place.

To accomplish what Ben Franklin challenges us to do, we must empower and develop everyone's capacity to collaborate with us and share in the leadership demands of the work. We must demonstrate vulnerability and humility when serving others and be open and available to listen to all suggestions and ideas. We must consistently show vision, inspiration, and courage when making the necessary decisions that have the potential to move us forward. We must stretch ourselves to think broadly about the impact of our actions on the entire learning community. All of these "musts" require a huge and unwavering trust and respect among all of the stakeholders involved in the process.

Ethical Dimensions of School Leadership

Exhibit 6.1 helps define the ethical implications of how values impact our attitudes, which ultimately explain our responses to situations. Leaders whose actions are congruent with what they say build the requisite conditions of trust and respect quickly to collectively drive the thoughts and actions of the learning community.

The bridge between a leader's moral judgment in decision making and resultant actions must be sturdy and strong. People can detect hypocrisy between the walk and the talk of a leader very quickly. Acting with integrity assumes that there is a wholeness or completeness that is considered when aligning these values, attitudes, and behaviors. Genuine and authentic behavior trumps popularity every time. It is the consistent call for attempting our very best each and every day that resonates with followers, and with this deeply rooted sense of moral purpose comes the courage to do the right things in the right way in educating our children.

EXHIBIT 6.1 Values, Attitudes, and Ethical Behavior

Value	Attitude	Ethical Behavior
Wisdom and knowledge	Experience promotes wisdom that supports converting information into knowledge.	Using knowledge to solve problems ethically and consistently do what is morally right.
Self-control	Self-control involves effectively managing and controlling reactions to challenging situations.	Putting personal motivations aside and acting with objectivity by doing what is moral and ethical.
Justice	Acting justly and fairly is a long-term driver of ethical behavior; remembering the "Golden Rule."	Establishing just and mutually agreed-upon expectations and consequences and administering them fairly to all people.
Transcendence	The belief in a power and source outside oneself reduces self-serving actions, increases humility, and acknowledges the greater good and the betterment of society.	Putting organizational and stakeholder interests above self interests. Identifying a personal purpose that is aligned with the shared mission.
Love and kindness	Treating people with caring and compassion helps increase the reservoir of positive affection and love.	Recognizing and encouraging others for their contributions.
Courage and integrity	Ethics requires the courage to do the right things consistently without regard to personal consequences.	Making some unpopular decisions based on fair consideration of the facts.

Elementary 25

Before inviting others to join the Elementary 25 team, I felt compelled to share my beliefs and values about teaching and learning, which at the time sounded something like this:

- I believe that all children can learn to significantly high levels given time, opportunity, and support.
- I believe that the welfare of children is our first priority as a society.
- I believe that children have a natural curiosity and an innate desire to learn and succeed.
- I believe a child's success has a significant influence on that child's sense of efficacy and self-esteem.
- I believe that children respond to a caring and nurturing learning environment.
- I believe in high academic and behavioral expectations for every child.
- I believe that meeting children's basic needs is vitally important before learning can take place.
- I believe teachers make the most difference in promoting learning.
- I believe teachers have the responsibility to build capacity in every child.
- I believe teachers must be lifelong learners and grow professionally to model the excitement of discovery.
- I believe that the school and the greater community have a commitment to develop not the just the mind but the whole child.

- I believe that education is successful when home, school, and the entire learning community partner to work together to benefit our children.
- I believe that education is the great equalizer and has an enormous impact on the potential quality of life of the entire society.

Personal statements such as these provide a transparency to the expectations of leadership. They disclose the nonnegotiables in the relationship between the leader and the learning community. My credibility and my authenticity as a school leader determined the extent to which this core team would willingly commit to the demands of extra doses of time, talent, energy, expertise, creativity, and support that were necessary to open Elementary 25 with a sense of purpose.

One of our biggest points of pride was that by most everyone's measuring stick, Elementary 25 met the mark in terms of the moral and ethical behavior that was consistently displayed by every adult and student every day. Our school-wide rule was easy to recall, but more difficult to follow: "Be in the right place, at the right time, doing the right thing, even when no one is looking." This simple statement represented the "rightness" of our decisions and choices even when there was no one there to judge us or apply a consequence. This simple sentiment provided the ethical principles and clear standards by which we lived at our little school.

We agreed as a staff not to focus on the typical character-word-of-the-month program that seemed to us to be more artificial and less authentic. Instead we emphasized the daily positive choices students and adults made and celebrated those positive choices publicly to ensure that everyone knew what our values looked like, sounded like, and felt like in action. Creating a school environment in which teaching and learning took place morally and ethically was an important challenge for us to master. I realized the responsibility for that challenge emanated from me as the school leader. My deep desire was to be a credible, moral, and servant leader, one who led with integrity, and shaped and strengthened everyone's commitment to respecting the ethical code we created. Our foundation of integrity evoked a sense of pride in our identity as a school; it generated a sense of teamwork and collaboration; it connected personal values with those of the school; it enhanced the attachment and commitment of everyone to these ethical standards; and it motivated us to display a positive attitude and effective effort to achieve great things. Our school motto, "Think you can, work hard, get smart," applied to all.

Key Ideas

- Who we are as people is determined by our beliefs, values, and attitudes.
- Our credibility as leaders is enhanced by the congruence between our values and our actions.
- Morality and ethical leadership are essential to our success as an educational institution and as a society.
- The values of honesty, respect, fairness, compassion, responsibility, and perseverance transcend cultures, religious beliefs, and other human orientations.
- Character education endorses excellence in living as well as excellence in learning.
- Moral purpose guides, directs, and acts as a catalyst for all of our work in teaching, learning, and leading.
- Servant leadership evolves from a core set of values that promotes leaders as caretakers and guardians of the needs and interests of those they serve.

Questions to Continue This Discussion

- Do present practices in your school support, neglect, or contradict the professed values and ethical aims of your system?
- How do schools recruit the help they need from the other key formative institutions that shape the values of our young, including families, faith communities, and the media?
- Do you view yourself as a servant leader? Why or why not?
- How does leadership set, model, and consistently enforce high standards of respect and responsibility to ensure a positive, cohesive moral culture at the building level?
- How does the increasing dysfunction of our society impact our schools? Where do we as leaders draw the line between assuming our responsibility to provide a moral compass for our students and teachers and letting others stand up and guide with a moral authority to do what is just and right?

CHAPTER SEVEN

The Change Leader: Advocating for All Learners

"Let us live so that when we come to die even the undertaker will be sorry."

MARK TWAIN

Education is not an island. It has always been affected by what our broader society thinks, believes, and does. But now, to a greater degree than at any time in our history, the political shifts, the social transformations, the economic ups and downs, the legal dimensions, and other cultural contexts all impact how schools conceive the future and prepare to respond to it, or, more hopefully, create and influence it. School leaders are called upon to anticipate and understand trends, sometimes to be a messenger for them, to act as a change agent to address them, and to lead the way to a reflective and resilient reaction to them. As a result of this newly emphasized function of leadership, we are required to enhance our ability to enter a diverse environment of other people's realities and experiences and advocate for their needs and interests in teaching and learning. That advocacy almost always implies change and reform.

Our current world is changing in ways that dramatically alter our previous assumptions, beliefs, traditions, and policies that historically served our American education system better than they do right now. Comparatively, we are losing ground with other nations that are proactively responding to this astounding rate and pace of change. Many of our traditions and institutions are lagging behind our global neighbors. Our education system is one of those that is impacted most by the pace of change. We react to change much more slowly and cautiously than other systems. To anticipate change, rather than react to it, organizations like schools must identify trends and examine their possible implications for our work. Again, as Mark Twain asserted, "There is no such thing as a new idea." We are experiencing the power and complexity of this simple statement each and every day in our schools and districts as we attempt to reform, rethink, renew, regain, refocus, reframe, revisit, retrain, reinvent, and reestablish practices that will support our efforts in educating our students to higher levels.

The National Association of Elementary School Principals (NAESP) published a provocative resource in 2008 titled *Vision 2021: Transformations in Leading, Learning and Community* (2008b). In it are forecasts of a future that requires new looks at tools and creative plans that will prepare our students and adults to be highly adaptive learners in this rapidly changing world. It behooves us as school leaders to heed these sometimes subtle, most times substantial influences on our work. NAESP mentions nine trends that will inform our thinking and help us identify and explore the challenges and opportunities that lie ahead.

- Schools are the learning portals to a global workplace. The new work will be more project-based, collaborative, and technologically oriented. This new workplace will become more globally competitive and will demand skills that require creative and innovative solutions.
- Free market forces create tensions between school choice and education equity. As our population continues to

become increasingly diverse, school leaders will need to advocate for the minority and immigrant populations to receive equitable resources to close the opportunity and achievement gaps.

- Hyperlinked learning explores meaning through multimedia. Technology will accelerate learning and make it more collaborative. Personalized learning capitalizing on individual interests and talents will become more commonplace. If embraced, technology can provide greater flexibility in delivering content, and, as a result, learners will be more fully engaged in learning it.

- Scientific knowledge and technology bring new understanding to child brain development. The ability to redefine and resequence teaching and learning pedagogy will customize and increase the access to knowledge.

- Holistic standards expand expectations for achieving student potential. The Common Core State Standards had not been created in 2008 when this report was written; however, the emphasis on accountability and the use of data to inform decision making is mentioned as an important consideration of quality and equity.

- Networks of learning innovation experiment with new learning strategies for children. Research, collaboration, and knowledge sharing will link schools to best practices.

- The surveillance society links school to electronic safety networks. The security and welfare of students and adults in schools will be enhanced as well as the potential for parents to monitor online activity and communication.

- Society's mounting debts compromise future investments in education. The competition for limited resources will increase and funds for education will require the public's ownership and affirmation of the importance of education to our democracy.

- Principals set the standards as lead advocates for learning. They will be charged with the responsibility to establish and sustain learning organizations that can potentially transform individual lives and communities.

Source: Adapted from National Association of Elementary School Principals, 2008b

Rather than predicting what the future will be, trends indicate directions of change and bring focus to what the future may look like. As educators, we must face some of the hard facts and realities of not paying attention to what the future has in store for us and how our responses, if not prudent, will limit our potential to regain our predominate and powerful leadership position in this different and interconnected world.

Facing Some Hard Facts

We are unaccustomed as a nation to finish in any place other than first in most world competitions. We are used to winning the proverbial blue ribbon in most of our performances. We do not know how to come from behind, since we are typically out in front. The auto industry taught us a very humbling lesson in the mid-1970s. Before then, our economy was substantially based upon manufacturing the automobile. A complacent and sleepy industry missed signs of what was happening in Japan and other nations, and failed to make the necessary changes to compete with them. Our automobile dominance was canceled in the relative blink of an eye.

Unless we face our education dilemma right here and right now, there is a strong likelihood that America will be overtaken in the realm of education and the effect the education level of our populace has on business the same way we were in our automobile plants, but with far more devastating results. The outflow of dollars to Japan for goods overwhelmed our economy 30 years ago. It is happening again. This time we are paying higher salaries to well-educated workers overseas for services, and our attempts to deflect the impact of this trend are currently unsuccessful. The goal to be the best-educated populace is out of our reach at the moment. The sooner we accept that fact, the sooner we can plan to do something constructive and proactive about it.

Reviews of test results from the Programme for International Student Assessment (PISA), administered through the Organisation for Economic Co-operation and Development (OECD), are disappointing at best. This exam is given every three years to 15-year-olds in nations across the globe—most recently in 2009 to students in 65 countries. Students from the United States performed at or slightly above the OECD average in reading, at the OECD average in science, and significantly below the OECD average in mathematics. Among the 34 OECD countries, the United States ranked 14th in reading, 17th in science, and 23rd in mathematics.

Data from the Trends in International Mathematics and Science Study (TIMSS, http://nces.ed.gov/timss/) are just as discouraging. They suggest that the relative international standing of U.S. students declines as they progress through our public school system. In both mathematics and science, our students perform above the international average in grade 4, close to the international average in grade 8, and considerably below it in grade 12. Our advanced placement students in grade 12 underperform as compared with other nations. The competition does not include Japan and other Asian countries that typically do well in mathematics and science because they do not take the exam as twelfth graders, so given that fact, the results are even more cause for concern.

The information in comprehensive reports from the National Center for Education Statistics (2009) can serve as a starting point for our discussions and efforts to define the components of an appropriate 21st-century world-class education and the necessary rigor that is demanded by readiness for life after high school in a global society. If the United States is to improve the teaching and learning of mathematics and science for all of its students, we must carefully examine not just how much other countries outrank us, but also how their policies and practices are different from ours and how those different policies help their students achieve better results. TIMSS shows us where U.S. education stands—not just in terms of test scores, but also in terms of what is included in our textbooks, taught in our schools, and learned by our students. Examination of these data provides a valuable opportunity to shed new light on education in the United States through the lens of other benchmark countries.

These consistently dismal results have led many researchers to conclude that the education system in our country is broken and has been for the past 30 years. We spend more than nearly every other country on K–12 education (http://www.oecd.org), and our performance is mediocre at best. Their advice is to make education reform a policy priority and rethink almost everything about how we go about accomplishing our educational goals. We are realizing that it is very difficult work to dramatically improve our schools, to close the pervasive achievement gap, and to raise the bar on our unimpressive student performance on international assessments. It requires commitment, focus, leadership, and resources. As school leaders, we are challenged to engage in policies that will support school success for all students. Jim Collins, author of *Good to Great* (2001), states that the only "organizations to improve are those where the truth is told and the brutal facts confronted." As educators, we need to confront those "brutal facts" and with resilience never before seen in our nation. We need to actively engage with and work to shape education policy to identify, influence, and invest in the issues, trends, and potential changes that will help to make our schools better.

What Is Resiliency?

The concept of resilience originated in research on child behavior, not far removed from our work as school leaders. Some children prove to be positive, persistent, focused, flexible, and proactive despite extremely challenging and stressful home environments and experiences. They overcome barriers to change and develop deep sources of adaptability and positive and hopeful responses to adversity. Their ability to recover, learn, and grow stronger is both courageous and inspiring. Their elastic reactions present energy and enthusiasm to any situation. I have had many opportunities to witness resilient students in action, and I am constantly amazed by their desire to move forward after bouncing back, displaying complete trust that the outcome they work so hard for will eventually be in their grasp and will be worth the trouble.

Educators need to learn from and model this resilient behavior in our overriding mission to serve all students well and ultimately heal our broken schools and districts. We are asked to confront challenges that our current system is not designed or equipped to handle. Some parts of our education system are so badly shattered that only radically different and potentially disruptive ideas will have a positive impact. These problems are not just dents in the system, they are gaping holes. The achievement gap between majority and minority populations, changing family structures, blatant poverty, reduced school budgets and resources, and shortages of qualified teachers, just to name a few issues, all require a revived and more intense resiliency on our parts. Yes, they are society's issues, but we need to help solve them. Motivation and expertise go hand in hand, because we learn about what we care about. In order to promote and advocate for the best for every learner, we need to look for and find an optimistic and hopeful future, and be willing to change to meet the demands that this future presents. Our ability as school leaders to bounce back from the negativity and pessimism that has surrounded our work lately will determine how quickly these necessary reforms to the system will occur.

Theories on Change

Effective school leaders are effective agents of improvement and change. They understand how to initiate the right change, support the people involved with the change, and modify or sustain the change over time. They learn how to ground their conversation in defensible arguments, how to make decisions and formulate actions and plans based upon a commitment to renewal and improvement, and how to appraise the consequences of their behavior and decisions. Now more than ever, the challenge of change, even the pain of change, will need to be tolerated and then embraced if we are to move ahead with our reform agenda.

Douglas Reeves, in his 2008 book, *Reframing Teacher Leadership*, describes a forecast that educators 20 years ago might have made about the lack of change we traditionally experience in our profession. It is disturbingly accurate today.

> Twenty years from now in a very large number of our schools, you really won't see much change. Desks in many schools will remain in rows while teachers lecture to students who are entirely disengaged. Grading policies will be about the same, as will schedules, credit hours, transcripts, and traditions such as final exams. Even though we know now, and will know 20 years from now, that these are terrible practices, we'll keep doing them anyway. We'll continue to assign teachers to courses based on per-

sonal preferences and tradition rather than student needs. We'll continue to have the same amount of time for every student to complete the task, even though we know that student learning needs and paces are different today and will be different 20 years from now. We have too many kids who are not reading on grade level today, and we'll have too many 20 years from now. We know the lifelong consequences of school failure today, and we'll be just about as indifferent to them 20 years from now. Legislators and school boards and superintendents can yell, threaten, test, and intimidate. They can do everything except change our professional practices. Sure, we'll have a lot more technology, but a lot of it will remain under the jurisdiction of the business and operations leadership of the district rather than instructional leadership—just the way it has been since the 1950s when the entire district had only one computer. We'll have a lot more computers 20 years from now, but the kids most likely to use them in pursuit of their education will be the same kids who have them today—that is, the economically advantaged kids who have computers at home anyway. Revolutionary change 20 years from now? Don't bet on it. (Reeves, 2008)

These predictions are pretty depressing, and, worse, they are probably correct. How are we going to confront this phenomenon of a high level of resistance to change—change that can possibly improve educational practice? But just as troubling as the resistance to change is the trend of adopting any and every change that comes down the pike without regard for whether it has any potential to support our work. Effective leaders discriminate among all of the policies, programs, and practices to find the candidates for good changes that help us solve the substantial problems that we are facing. Our responsibility to effect positive policy change is undeniably critical.

Why do most change initiatives fail? Experts on systemic change offer their ideas about why our success rate is so low. John Kotter (2008) says, "Based on the analysis of about 100 efforts in organizations to produce large-scale change—i.e. implementing new growth strategies, putting in new IT systems, reorganizing to reduce expenses—we found that in over 70 percent of the situations where substantial changes were clearly needed, either they were not fully launched, or the change efforts failed, or changes were achieved but over-budget, late, and with great frustration." Michael Fullan (2001) asserts, "Single-factor theories of change are doomed to failure." John Goodlad (Goldberg, 2000) explains, "No model of reform recommended by serious reformers has ever made it to the showroom floor. By the time the school staff, local authorities, teacher associations, and politicians get through with it, a reform plan is only a pale shadow of its original form." Senge and his associates (1999) offer, "The fundamental flaw in most innovators' strategies is that they focus on their innovations, on what they are trying to do, rather than on understanding how the larger culture, structures and norms will react to their efforts." Seemingly insurmountable challenges, right? There is better news.

The following representative researchers help us understand the complexities and nuances of good changes to better fulfill our responsibilities for initiating them. Following are some of their informed recommendations for overcoming the barriers to change that exist in every school and district and guaranteeing that the right changes are considered and then led.

John Kotter

- Establish a sense of urgency.
- Create a guiding coalition.
- Develop a vision and strategy.
- Communicate the change vision.
- Empower broad-based action.
- Generate short-term wins.

- Consolidate gains, producing more change.
- Anchor new approaches in the culture.

Source: Adapted from Kotter, 1996

Michael Fullan

- Love your employees.
- Connect peers with purpose.
- Capacity building prevails.
- Learning is the work.
- Transparency rules.
- Systems learn.

Source: Adapted from Fullan, 2008

Ben Levin

- Set high expectations and clear goals that are understood by all.
- Have few and highly focused goals that can deliver better outcomes.
- Reduce inequity and increase public confidence.
- Communicate frequently and respectfully to promote engagement with stakeholders.
- Align the goals to policies and programs that matter.
- Build the capacity at every level to achieve the goals.

Source: Adapted from Levin, 2008

Charles Reigeluth

- Initiate a system change effort.
- Prepare a starter team.
- Develop a district-wide framework and capacity for change.
- Create designs for new schools.
- Implement and evolve the new system.

Source: Adapted from Reigeluth, 2006

There are no profound or new insights or suggestions here or in any of the resources on change theory; just common-sense statements about how to avoid the likelihood that our attempts at educational change will fail. There is a plethora of change readiness research and leaders need to become familiar with the guidance and advice that these experts and others offer to inform our improvement efforts.

Educational Leadership Policy Standards: ISLLC 2008

School leaders are committed to the democratic principles underlying American public school systems. As a matter of fact, in many states we take an oath to uphold them. We are to actively engage with and work to shape educational policy so it reflects that dedication to equity for the diverse learners in our buildings and districts. We are obliged to lead ongoing dialogue with our learning communities to identify, influence, and respond to issues, trends, and potential changes that will improve the achievement outcomes in our schools. *ISLLC 2008* Standard 6, the final policy standard, emphasizes our responsibility to maintain a current familiarity with education policy and assume a proactive position in advocating for all students.

> **Standard 6:** An education leader promotes the success of every student by understanding, responding to, and influencing the political, social, economic, legal, and cultural context.
>
> **Functions:**
> - Advocate for children, families, and caregivers.
> - Act to influence local, district, state, and national decisions affecting student learning.

> - Assess, analyze, and anticipate emerging trends and initiatives in order to adapt leadership strategies.
>
> Source: Council of Chief State School Officers, 2008

The assumptions made in Standard 6 define our role as informed policy analysts at the local, state, and national levels. Decisions that impact the opportunities and success of our students are ours to initiate and influence. Educational excellence and equity are the priorities that we pursue with intention and intensity. We grow our skills as communicators to ensure our school community has accurate and timely information about our school's performance. We not only serve as advocates for our students and families, but also as stewards of our mission to strengthen and improve the entire public school system.

Common Core State Standards: From Common Sense to Common Practice

The 2011/12 school year represented the formal launch of the Common Core State Standards initiative in many of the adopting states and territories. It is the source of much angst and hand wringing, but also of great anticipation and excitement to discuss what the educational fuss is all about. Not since 1983 and the release of the *Nation at Risk* report by the National Commission on Excellence in Education have we had such powerful and passionate discussions about the future of teaching and learning in America. I believe the reason for some of this emotional intensity and frustration in our conversations could be that we are still talking about relatively the same issues that we were concerned about in 1983.

Yes, we are still at risk. The data prove that. Actually, many educational experts believe that we have lost significant ground in our battle against mediocrity since 1983. My first principalship began in that same year and the realization that we are still addressing similar concerns about educational equity and excellence three decades later is very disconcerting to me and illustrates how slowly change migrates into our system. The sense of urgency that was conveyed in the *Nation At Risk* report has done little to mobilize us to find solutions to the myriad challenges we faced then and continue to face now in achieving quality education for all of our students.

But all that could change, and I am optimistic that it will. I believe we are very capable of identifying and defining our difficulties; we know the daunting scope of our problems; we are even aware of some very logical solutions to them. Our barrier to change is that we do not push hard enough when we have these rare opportunities to reboot our system to determine what is essential for high performance in teaching and learning. More than 90 percent of our states and territories have taken the first step toward exploring the reform prospects by adopting the Common Core State Standards (CCSS). That percentage certainly represents a critical mass of membership in this transformational effort. This is our chance to prove that we can thoughtfully engage in this work and really make a positive difference for our students and, in the long run, our nation.

The implications of the new Common Core State Standards are both exciting and overwhelming. Standards do not tell teachers how to teach and cannot by themselves ensure the quality of our nation's education system. However, they constitute an important starting point in helping schools determine the knowledge and skills that all students must have to be successful after high school in careers, college, and life. States, districts, schools, and teachers need to begin planning now for how the new standards will impact what is currently happening in America's schools and classrooms. Using some of the tools and recommendations in this chapter might help focus the conversations and sustain the improvement intentions of the CCSS.

So here we are at the crossroads of taking the Common Core State Standards to the next level, one that will directly impact teaching and learning in our nation's classrooms. The heavy lifting is just beginning. The process starts with the courageous conviction, relentless faith, and pervasive wisdom of every professional educator who potentially can bring relevance as well as reality to the proposed reform. That is the only way the CCSS will be viewed as a viable initiative and not another failed attempt to improve our educational system. If the core planning team at Elementary 25 were still in existence, and if I were a gambling girl, I would put all my money on their ability to complete the thoughtful implementation of the CCSS as well as they did the opening of a benchmark school. That team and teams like it across the country are up to the challenging task of translating the Common Core State Standards from common sense to common practice.

Elementary 25

This is my last opportunity to highlight and celebrate the wonderful work that was accomplished by 10 amazingly dedicated and talented individuals who morphed into one incredibly dedicated and talented core planning team for Elementary 25. It is also my final chance to offer hope and optimism for the future of educational reform in our nation. It can be done. I had the privilege of watching reform evolve through the innocent eyes of students, the trusting eyes of parents, and the compassionate eyes of teachers. Together we basically created a school building from dirt, a shared vision from wishes and dreams, a research- and standards-based instructional program from a blank page. We created a moral and ethical school culture from a community's deeply held convictions of what a great learning environment should expect from and honor about both its students and its adults. This feat was a point of pride for our entire state.

In a pervasive climate of accountability and compliance, we succeeded through our own collective and then extended conversations at doing what was necessary to create an extremely high-performing learning community—by any standard. We accepted the challenge to hold our students and ourselves to a higher expectation of performance than was mandated. We set our goals above and beyond what was demanded. We chose to accept responsibility for all of our choices and about everything we valued at Elementary 25.

In the end, we collaboratively designed, defined, and developed a high-performing elementary school that was recognized as a welcoming and happy place filled with learning, laughter, encouraging words, questions, answers, passion, and power. Everyone protected and nurtured each other, cared for each other, and respected each other's contributions for what we had created.

For teaching and learning to flourish in every school as it did at Elementary 25, educators, parents, community leaders, and policymakers must agree on what needs to be achieved in our nation's schools, what can be solved here, and what can be potentially abandoned here. It will demand strong and shared leadership that is visionary, collaborative, culturally sensitive, resourceful, moral and ethical, and, most important, leadership that respects that learning is at the center of our work as educators.

Key Ideas

- The larger cultural context, including the political, social, economic, and legal dimensions of society, dramatically affects education.

- Effective school leaders anticipate trends to help create and influence a better future for all.
- Student performance data in the United States show that educators must face and accept some hard facts that as a nation we no longer have the best-educated populace in the world and as leaders we need to respond quickly to mediate this educational crisis.
- Resiliency as a leadership skill will assume a more important role in the daily functions we perform as we work through the challenges of leading a school to greatness.
- Effective school leaders must understand the change process to manage it and support people through it to have substantive success with school reform initiatives.
- The implementation of the Common Core State Standards is the most significant organizational change and education reform that school leaders will address for the next several years.

Questions to Continue This Discussion

- What do you believe you can do to ensure the success of all students by influencing the larger contexts in which we live and work?
- How do you engage in the political, social, economic, and legal aspects of leadership to promote the welfare of all students?
- What are your experiences in leading a change effort? Was it successful? Why or why not?
- Name some characteristics of resiliency that you could develop or refine in your leadership role. How would they contribute to your enhanced leadership performance?

- Where is your school or district with plans to implement the Common Core State Standards? What is your role in advocating for these standards as a viable reform initiative to ensure educational excellence and equity for all students?

References and Suggested Reading

Allison, E., Besser, L., Campsen, L., Cordova, J., Doubek, B., Gregg, L., … White, M. (2010). *Data teams: The big picture.* Englewood, CO: Lead + Learn Press.

Allison, E., Clinton, J., Hattie, J., Kamm, C., Lassiter, C., McNulty, B. A., … White, S. (2011). *Activate: A leader's guide to people, practices, processes.* Englewood, CO: Lead + Learn Press.

Almeida, L., Benson, L., Christinson, J., Doubek, B., Howard, L., Mascorro, L., … Wiggs, M. (2011). *Standards and assessment: The core of quality instruction.* Englewood, CO: Lead + Learn Press.

Barth, R. S. (2001). *Learning by heart.* San Francisco, CA: Jossey-Bass.

Barth, R. S. (2002, May). The culture builder. *Educational Leadership, 59*(8), 6–11.

Bennis, W. (1994). *On becoming a leader.* Cambridge, MA: Perseus.

Blankstein, A. M. (2010). *Failure is not an option: Six principles for making student success the only option.* Thousand Oaks, CA: Corwin.

Bolman, L. G., & Deal, T. E. (1995). *Leading with soul: An uncommon journey of spirit.* San Francisco, CA: Jossey-Bass.

Bonstingl, J. J. (2001). *Schools of quality* (3rd ed.). Thousand Oaks, CA: Corwin.

Boyer, E. L. (1995). *The basic school: A community for learning.* San Francisco, CA: Jossey-Bass.

Cashman, K. (1998). *Leadership from the inside out: Becoming a leader for life.* Provo, UT: Executive Excellence Publishing.

Cohen, J. (2006, Summer). Social, emotional, ethical and academic education: Creating a climate for learning, participation in democracy and well-being. *Harvard Educational Review, 76*(2), 201–237.

Collins, J. (2001). *Good to great: Why some companies make the leap and others don't.* New York, NY: HarperCollins Publishing.

Common Core. (2009). *Why we're behind: What top nations teach their students but we don't*. Washington, DC: Author. Retrieved from http://www.commoncore.org/_docs/CCreport_whybehind.pdf

Common Core State Standards Initiative. (n.d.). *Standards-setting considerations*. Retrieved from www.corestandards.org/assets/Considerations.pdf

Council of Chief State School Officers. (2008). *Educational leadership policy standards: ISLLC 2008*. Washington, DC: Author. Retrieved from http://www.ccsso.org/Documents/2008/Educational_Leadership_Policy_Standards_2008.pdf

Covey, S. R. (1990). *Principle-centered leadership*. New York, NY: Summit Books.

Covey, S. R. (2004). *The 8th habit: From effectiveness to greatness*. New York: Simon and Schuster.

Darling-Hammond, L. (1997). *The right to learn: A blueprint for creating schools that work*. New York, NY: John Wiley and Sons.

Darling-Hammond, L. (2010a). *The flat world and education: How America's commitment to equity will determine our future*. New York, NY: Teachers College Press.

Darling-Hammond, L. (2010b). *Performance counts: Assessment systems that support high-quality learning*. Washington, DC: Council of Chief State School Officers.

Deal, T. E., & Peterson, K. D. (1999). *Shaping school culture: The heart of leadership*. San Francisco, CA: Jossey-Bass.

Deming, W. E. (2000). *Out of the crisis* (rev. ed.). Cambridge, MA: MIT Press.

Drucker, P. (1990). *Managing the non-profit organization*. New York, NY: HarperCollins.

DuFour, R., DuFour, R., & Eaker, R. (2008). *Revisiting professional learning communities at work: New insights for improving schools*. Bloomington, IN: Solution Tree Press.

DuFour, R., & Eaker, R. (1998). *Professional learning communities at work: Best practices for enhancing student achievement*. Bloomington, IN: Solution Tree Press.

DuFour, R., & Marzano, R. J. (2010). *Leaders of learning: How district, school, and classroom leaders improve student achievement*. Bloomington, IN: Solution Tree Press.

Dunkle, C. (2012). *Leading the Common Core State Standards: From common sense to common practice*. Thousand Oaks, CA: Corwin.

Dweck, C. (2008). *Mindset: The new psychology of success*. New York, NY: Ballentine.

Elmore, R. (Ed.). (2011). *I used to think …, and now I think …: Twenty leading educators reflect on the work of school reform*. Cambridge, MA: Harvard Education Press.

Fullan, M. (2001). *Leading in a culture of change*. San Francisco, CA: Jossey-Bass.

Fullan, M. (2008). *The six secrets of change*. Retrieved from www.michaelfullan.ca/resource_assets/.../08_Nov_Keynote_A4.pdf

Fullan, M. (2010). *The moral imperative realized*. Thousand Oaks, CA: Corwin.

Garmston, R. (1997, Fall). Can collaboration be taught? *Journal of Staff Development, 18*(4).

Garmston, R., & Wellman, B. (2009). *The adaptive school: A sourcebook for developing collaborative groups* (2nd ed.). Norwood, MA: Christopher-Gordon.

Goldberg, M. F. (2000, September). Leadership for change: An interview with John Goodlad. *Phi Delta Kappan, 82*(1), 82–85. Retrieved from www.eric.ed.gov/ERICWebPortal/recordDetail?accno=EJ612902

Gruenert, S. (2008, March/April). School culture and school climate: They are not the same thing. *Principal Magazine*, 56–59. Retrieved from http://www.naesp.org/resources/2/Principal/2008/M-Ap56.pdf

Guskey, T. R. (2000). *Evaluating professional development*. Thousand Oaks, CA: Corwin Press.

Guskey, T. R. (2002). Professional development and teacher change. *Teachers and Teaching, 8*(3), 381–391. Retrieved from *academic.research .microsoft.com/Paper/5985521.aspx?viewType=1*

Guskey, T. R. (2003). How classroom assessments improve learning. *Educational Leadership, 60*(5), 6–11.

Hale, E. L., & Moorman, H. N. (2003). *Preparing school principals: A national perspective on policy and program innovations.* Washington, DC: Institute for Educational Leadership.

Harvard Graduate School of Education. (2011, February). *Pathways to prosperity: Meeting the challenge of preparing young Americans for the 21st century.* Cambridge, MA: Author. Retrieved from http://www.gse.harvard.edu/news_events/features/2011/Pathways _to_Prosperity_Feb2011.pdf

Hattie, J. A. (2009). *Visible learning: A synthesis of over 800 meta-analyses relating to achievement.* New York, NY: Routledge.

Hayes-Jacobs, H. (2010). *Curriculum 21: Essential education for a changing world.* Alexandria, VA: ASCD.

Hobby, R. (2004). *A culture for learning: An investigation into the values and beliefs associated with effective schools.* Hay Group. Retrieved from http://transforminglearning.co.uk/homepage/Culture_for_Learning _Report.pdf

Institute for Educational Leadership. (2000). *Leadership for student learning: Reinventing the principalship.* Washington, DC: Author. Retrieved from http://www.iel.org/programs/21st/reports/principal.pdf

Jerald, C. D. (2006, December). *School culture: "The hidden curriculum"* (Issue Brief). Washington, DC: The Center for Comprehensive School Reform and Improvement.

Kearney, K. (Ed.). (2003). *Moving leadership standards into everyday work: Descriptions of practice.* San Francisco, CA: WestEd.

Kotter, J. (1996). *Leading change.* Boston, MA: Harvard Business Press.

Kotter, J. (2008). *A sense of urgency.* Boston, MA: Harvard Business Press.

Kouzes, J. M., & Posner, B. Z. (2010). *The truth about leadership: The no-fads, heart of the matter facts you need to know.* San Francisco, CA: Jossey-Bass.

Lambert, L. (1998). *Building leadership capacity in schools.* Alexandria, VA: ASCD.

Lambert, L. (2002, May). A framework for shared leadership. *Educational Leadership, 59*(8), 94–95.

Leithwood, K., Seashore-Louis, K., Anderson, S., & Wahlstrom, K. (2004). *How leadership influences student learning.* New York, NY: The Wallace Foundation. Retrieved from http://www.wallacefoundation.org/knowledge-center/school-leadership/key-research/Pages/How-Leadership-Influences-Student-Learning.aspx

Levin, B. (2008). *How to change 5000 schools.* Boston, MA: Harvard University Press.

Lickona, T. (1993, November). The return of character education. *Educational Leadership, 51*(3), 6–11.

Littky, D. (with Grabelle, S.). (2004). *The big picture: Education is everyone's business.* Alexandria, VA: ASCD.

Marzano, R. (2003). *What works in schools: Translating research into action.* Alexandria, VA: ASCD.

Marzano, R. (2007). *The art and science of teaching: A comprehensive framework for effective instruction.* Alexandria, VA: ASCD.

Marzano, R., Pickering, D., & Pollock, J. (2001). *Classroom instruction that works: Research-based strategies for increasing student achievement.* Alexandria, VA: ASCD.

Marzano, R., Waters, T., & McNulty, B. (2005). *School leadership that works: From research to results.* Alexandria, VA: ASCD.

McKinsey and Company. (2010). *How the world's most improved school systems keep getting better.* Retrieved from http://www.mckinsey.com/clientservice/Social_Sector/our_practices/Education/Knowledge_Highlights/How%20School%20Systems%20Get%20Better.aspx

McNulty, B. A., & Besser, L. (2011). *Leaders make it happen! An administrator's guide to data teams.* Englewood, CO: Lead + Learn Press.

McTighe, J., Elliott, S., & Wiggins, G. (2004, September). You can teach for meaning. *Educational Leadership, 62*(1), 26–30.

Morgan, J. E. (1936). *Horace Mann: His ideas and ideals.* Washington, DC: National Home Library Foundation.

National Association of Elementary School Principals. (2008a). *Leading learning communities: Standards for what principals should know and be able to do* (2nd ed.). Executive summary retrieved from www.naesp.org/resources/1/Pdfs/LLC2-ES.pdf

National Association of Elementary School Principals. (2008b). *Vision 2021: Transformations in Leading, Learning and Community.* Alexandria, VA: Author.

National Association of Secondary School Principals. (2004). *Breaking ranks II: Strategies for leading high school reform.* Providence, RI: The Education Alliance.

National Center for Education Statistics. (2009). *The Nation's Report Card.* Retrieved from http://nces.ed.gov/nationsreportcard/

National Center for Urban School Transformation. (2011). *Improving climate and culture in urban schools.* Retrieved from www.ncust.org/ppts/Climate-and-Culture-2.ppt

National Commission on Excellence in Education. (1983, April). *A nation at risk: The imperative for educational reform.* Report to the United States Department of Education. Washington, DC: Author.

National Governors Association, Council of Chief State School Officers, & Achieve. (2008). *Benchmarking for success: Ensuring U.S. students receive a world-class education.* Washington, DC: Authors. Retrieved from http://www.achieve.org/BenchmarkingforSuccess

Northouse, P. (2007). *Leadership: Theory and practice.* Thousand Oaks, CA: Sage.

Organisation for Economic Co-operation and Development (OECD). (2010). *PISA 2009 results: Executive summary.* Retrieved from http://www.oecd.org/dataoecd/34/60/46619703.pdf

Organisation for Economic Co-operation and Development (OECD). (2011). *Strong performers and successful reformers in education: Lessons from PISA for the United States.* OECD Publishing. Retrieved from http://www.oecd.org/dataoecd/32/50/46623978.pdf

Pashler, H., Bain, P. M., Bottge, B. A., Graesser, A., Koedinger, K., McDaniel, M., & Metcalfe, J. (2007). *Organizing instruction and study to improve student learning (NCER 2007-2004)*. Washington, DC: National Center for Education Research, Institute of Education Sciences, U.S. Department of Education. Retrieved from http://ncer.ed.gov

Peters, T. J. (2010). *The little big things: 163 ways to pursue excellence.* New York, NY: Harper Studio.

Peterson, K. D. (2002). Positive or negative. *Journal of Staff Development, 23*(3), 10–14. Retrieved from www.learningforward.org/news/getDocument.cfm?articleID=430

Peterson, K. D., & Deal, T. E. (1998, September). How leaders influence the culture of schools. *Educational Leadership, 56*(1), 28–30.

Phillips, G., & Wagner, C. (2003). *School culture assessment.* Vancouver, BC: Mitchell Press, Agent 5 Design.

Pink, D. (2009). *Drive: The surprising truth about what motivates us.* New York, NY: Riverhead Books.

Porter, A. C., Murphy, J. F., Goldring, E. B., & Elliot, S. N. (2006). *Vanderbilt assessment of leadership in education.* Nashville, TN: Vanderbilt University.

Programme for International Student Assessment. (2009). Comparing countries' and economies' performance. In *What students know and can do: Student performance in reading, mathematics and science.* Organisation for Economic Co-operation and Development. Retrieved from www.pisa.oecd.org/dataoecd/54/12/46643496.pdf

Reeves, D. B. (2000). *Accountability in action: A blueprint for learning organizations.* Englewood, CO: Advanced Learning Centers.

Reeves, D. B. (2002a). *Holistic accountability: Serving students, schools, and community.* Thousand Oaks, CA: Corwin.

Reeves, D. B. (2002b). *The leader's guide to standards: A blueprint for educational equity and excellence.* San Francisco, CA: Jossey-Bass.

Reeves, D. B. (2004). *Accountability for learning: How teachers and school leaders can take charge.* Alexandria, VA: ASCD.

Reeves, D. B. (2006). *The learning leader: How to focus school improvement for better results.* Alexandria, VA: ASCD.

Reeves, D. B. (2008). *Reframing teacher leadership to improve your school.* Alexandria, VA: ASCD.

Reeves, D. B. (2009a). *Assessing educational leaders: Evaluating performance for improved individual and organizational results* (2nd ed.). Thousand Oaks, CA: Corwin.

Reeves, D. B. (2009b). *Leading change in your school: How to conquer myths, build commitment, and get results.* Alexandria, VA: ASCD.

Reeves, D. B. (2010a, January). Getting ready for national standards. *ASCD Express, 5*(8).

Reeves. D. B. (2010b). *Transforming professional development into student results.* Alexandria, VA: ASCD.

Reeves, D. B. (2011). *Finding your leadership focus: What matters most for student results.* New York, NY: Teachers College Press.

Reigeluth, C. (2006, March). The guidance system for transforming education. *TechTrends: Linking Research and Practice to Improve Learning, 50*(2), 41–51.

Robinson, V. M., Lloyd, C. A., & Rowe, K. J. (2008). The impact of leadership on student outcomes: An analysis of the differential effects of leadership types. *Educational Administration Quarterly, 44*(5), 635–674.

Sanders, N. M., & Simpson, J. (2005). *State policy framework to develop highly qualified educational administrators.* Washington, DC: The Council of Chief State School Officers.

Saphier, J., & King, M. (1985, March). Good seeds grow in strong cultures. *Educational Leadership, 42*(6), 67–74.

Schmoker, M. (2006). *Results now: How we can achieve unprecedented improvement in teaching and learning.* Alexandria, VA: ASCD.

Schmoker, M. (2011). *Focus: Elevating the essentials to radically improve student learning.* Alexandria, VA: ASCD.

Senge, P. (2006). *The fifth discipline: The art and practice of the learning organization* (2nd ed.). New York, NY: Doubleday.

Senge, P., Kleiner, A., Roberts, C., Ross, R., Roth, G., & Smith, B. (1999). *The dance of change.* New York, NY: Doubleday.

Sergiovanni, T. (2000). *The lifeworld of leadership: Creating culture, community and personal meaning in our schools.* San Francisco, CA: Jossey-Bass.

Spears, L. C. (1996). Reflections on Robert K. Greenleaf and servant leadership. *Leadership & Organization Development Journal, 17*(7), 33–35.

Speck, M., & Knipe, C. (2005). *Why can't we get it right? Designing high-quality professional development for standards-based schools.* Thousand Oaks, CA: Corwin.

Stiggins, R. (2005). *Student-involved assessment for learning* (4th ed.). Upper Saddle River, NJ: Prentice Hall.

Stiggins, R. (2006). *Balanced assessment systems: Redefining excellence in assessment.* Princeton, NJ: Educational Testing Service.

Tomlinson, C. A. (1999). *The differentiated classroom: Responding to the needs of all learners.* Alexandria, VA: ASCD.

Toye, C., Blank, R. K., Sanders, N., & Williams, A. (2006). *Key state education policies on PK-12 education.* Washington, DC: Council of Chief State School Officers.

U.S. Department of Education. (2008, April). *A nation accountable: Twenty-five years after a nation at risk.* Washington, DC: Author. Retrieved from http://www2.ed.gov/rschstat/research/pubs/accountable/accountable.pdf

U. S. Department of Education. (2010, March). *A blueprint for reform: The reauthorization of the elementary and secondary education act.* Washington, DC: Author. Retrieved from http://www2.ed.gov/policy/elsec/leg/blueprint/publicationtoc.html

Van der Post, L., & Taylor, J. (1986). *Testament to the Bushmen.* London, England: Penguin.

Wallace Foundation. (2006). *Leadership for learning: Making the connections among state, district, and school policies and practices.* New York, NY: Author.

Wallace Foundation. (2007). *Education leadership: A bridge to school reform.* New York, NY: Author.

Wallace Foundation. (2012). *The school principal as leader: Guiding schools to better teaching and learning.* New York, NY: Author.

Wheatley, M., & Kellner-Rogers, M. (1996). *A simpler way.* San Francisco, CA: Berrett-Kohler.

Whitaker, T. (2002). *What great principals do differently: 15 things that matter most.* Larchmont, NY: Eye on Education.

White, S. (2009). *Leadership maps.* Englewood, CO: Lead + Learn Press.

White, S. (2011a). *Beyond the numbers: Making data work for teachers and school leaders* (2nd ed.). Englewood, CO: Lead + Learn Press.

White, S. (2011b). *Show me the proof!: Tools and strategies to make data work with the Common Core State Standards* (2nd ed.). Englewood, CO: Lead + Learn Press.

Whitehurst, G. (2009). *Don't forget curriculum.* Washington, DC: Brookings Institution. Retrieved from http://www.brookings.edu/research/papers/2009/10/14-curriculum-whitehurst

Wiggins, G. (1998). *Educative assessment: Designing assessments to inform and improve student performance.* San Francisco, CA: Jossey-Bass.

Wiggins, G., & McTighe, J. (2005). *Understanding by design* (2nd ed.). Alexandria, VA: ASCD.

Williamson, R., & Blackburn, B. (2010). *Rigorous schools and classrooms: Leading the way.* Larchmont, NY: Eye On Education.

Wiseman, L. (with McKeown, G.). (2010). *Multipliers: How the best leaders make everyone smarter.* New York, NY: HarperCollins.

Index

Accountability, xxiv, 11, 27, 28, 44, 46, 57, 59, 68, 73, 74, 77, 83, 88, 116
   collective, 70
   developing, 43, 90
Achievement, 37, 40, 54, 73, 78, 89, 103
   challenge/change and, 12
   gap in, 14, 103, 107
   improving, 21, 61, 62, 66, 88
   student, xxii, 14, 17, 18, 21, 39, 44, 50, 66, 69, 70, 72, 84
Action, 24, 32, 91
   broad-based, 110
   collective, 22
   vision and, 28
Assessing Educational Leaders (Reeves), 16
Assessments, 8, 15, 29, 43, 63, 65, 69
Attitudes, 92, 94, 95 (exh.), 98
   compassionate/caring, 87
   modeling/nurturing, 38–39

Barth, Roland, 25, 42
Basic School: A Community for Learning, The (Boyer), 29, 87
Behavior, 16, 17, 61, 92, 94, 107, 108
   authentic, 94
   changing, 37
   ethical, 4, 19, 64, 88, 90, 95 (exh.), 97
   expectations for, 96
   learning and, 41
   moral/ethical, xxv, 4, 64, 97
   patterns of, 37
Beliefs, 16, 50, 96, 98
Bennis, Warren, 53, 92
Besser, Laura, 76–77
Blanchard, Ken, 92
Block, Peter, 92
Boyer, Ernest, 29, 87
Breaking Ranks II: Strategies for Leading High School Reform (NASSP), 10

Center for Improving School Culture, 44
Change, 39, 66, 101, 117
   agents, 15, 108
   capacity for, 111
   complexities/nuances of, 110

   leadership and, 52, 56, 117
   modifying/sustaining, 108
   rate/pace of, 102
   resistance to, 109
   theories on, 108–112
Character, 59
   education, 87–88, 98
Citizenship, 86, 87
Climate, 42, 50, 87
   culture and, 38–41
   positive, 49
Collaboration, xxi, xxii, 4, 13, 18, 29, 48, 58, 61, 63, 67, 68, 69, 75, 82, 91, 98, 102, 103, 116
   basic skills of, 71
   culture of, 43
   Data Teams and, 83–84
   definition of, 72
   effective, 73, 81
   impact of, 22
   improving, 37, 39
   inquiry and, 74
   motivation for, 80
   professional, 45, 71
   promoting, xxiv–xxv, 85
   teaching, 70–72, 84
Collins, Jim, 26, 106
Commitment, 28, 39, 53, 68, 72, 88–89
   shared, 11, 21, 69
Common Core State Standards (CCSS), xxv, 103, 113–115
   implementing, 117, 118
Common School Journal, 85
Communication, 15, 17, 22, 25, 33, 39, 59, 65, 92, 111
   deep, 71
   monitoring, 103
   open, 46
   oral/written, 10
   positive, 40
Community, xxv, 20, 24, 27, 59, 88, 113
   building, 64, 87, 93
   engaging, 9
   growth of, 46
   leadership and, 51

Compliance, 58, 88–89, 116
Council of Chief State School Officers (CCSSO), xxi, xxii, 7, 20
Covey, Stephen, 52, 53, 77, 91
Culture, xxii, 14, 16, 36, 46, 48, 50, 73, 81, 101, 112
   business of, 49
   climate and, 38–41
   collaborative, 79
   education and, 116
   healthy, 42
   high-performing, 4, 40, 83
   leadership and, 42
   new approaches to, 111
   one size fits all, 44–45
   power, 38
   purpose/meaning of, 3
   shaping, 42, 70
   sustaining, 8
   trusting/protective, 27
   See also School culture
Curriculum, 15, 29, 43, 63, 69, 81
   coherence of, 50
   learning and, 58
   standards-based, xxii, 4

Data, 47, 63, 80, 91
   cause and effect, xxv
   decision making and, 11, 58, 66, 75
   learning/teaching and, 90
   performance, 117
   quality management and, 59
   using, 23, 70, 76–77
Data Teams, 75–77, 83–84
   process for, 76 (exh.)
Deal, Terrence, 39, 40, 41, 56
Decision making, 17, 33, 46, 55, 71, 91, 93, 103, 108
   data and, 11, 58, 66, 75
   leadership and, 88
   moral/legal consequences of, 90
   ownership for, 72
Deming, W. Edwards, 53, 58
Development, 8, 9, 10, 14, 31, 77
   brain, 103
   leadership, 17, 43, 48
   professional, 7, 11, 15, 47, 63, 70, 75
Drive: The Surprising Truth about What Motivates Us (Pink), 77
Drucker, Peter, 53, 92

DuFour, Richard, 69–70
Dweck, Carol, 78, 79

Education, xxiii, 2, 36, 68, 80, 94, 106
   character, 87–88, 98
   commitment to, 53, 103
   culture and, 116
   democracy and, 104
   dilemmas in, 104–105
   ethics and, 86
   improving, 79, 83, 109
   moral nature and, 85
   policy, 107, 112
   quality of life and, 97
   society and, 101
   standards-based, 32
Educational Leadership Policy Standards: ISLLC 2008 (CCSSO), xxi, 6–8, 20, 22–24, 43–45, 59–62, 80–81, 89–91, 112
Elementary 25: 26, 27, 28, 29, 30, 45–48, 59, 62–65, 81–83, 96–98, 115–116
   culture of, 46
   described, 24–25
   planning experience for, 65
Equity, 87, 90, 102, 103, 113, 114
Ethics, 86, 88, 89, 90, 92, 93, 97, 98, 99
Excellence, 58, 64, 83, 98, 113, 114
Expectations, 43, 45, 46, 71, 91, 111

Faith-based organizations, 88, 93
Family unit, breakdown of, 87, 107
Feedback, 12, 77, 79
Focus, 15, 39, 64, 76, 104
Franklin, Ben, 93–94
Fullan, Michael, 42, 88, 89, 110, 111

Garmston, Robert, 70
Goals, 9, 40, 53, 70, 71, 81, 106, 111, 116
   challenging, 47, 80
   collective, 21, 53
   long-term, 64
   meeting, 23, 28
   short-term, 93
"Good Seeds Grow in Strong Cultures" (Saphier and King), 45
Good to Great (Collins), 106
Goodlad, John: on reform, 110

Greenleaf, Robert: servant leadership and, 91
Growth, 46, 77, 79
  personal/spiritual, 61, 93
  professional, 8, 43, 61, 93, 96

Half, Robert, 2
Hattie, John, 72, 73
Hay Group Education, 48
Heinlein, Robert, 2
Hobby, Russell: on culture, 48
Honesty, 46, 86, 98
Hope, 5–6, 47, 68, 115

Implementation Audit, 61, 62, 66
Improvement, 38, 40, 46, 47, 48, 49, 77, 108, 112
  accountability for, 69, 83
  continuous, xxv, 23, 59, 70
  determining, 27
  efforts for, 18, 39
  fostering, 12
  goal of, 70
  influencing, 48
  researching, 18
  school, xxv, 42, 44, 49, 70
  sustainable, 23, 27
Information, 62, 64, 80
  distribution of, 72
  inquiry-based use of, 13
Inquiry, xxii, 18, 71, 83, 91
  collaboration and, 74
  data-driven, 77
Institute for Educational Leadership (IEL), 10–11
Instruction, xxiv, 15, 29, 61, 63
  developing, 12, 43
  quality, 44, 60
  research-/standards-based, 115–116
Integration, xxii, 8, 72, 83
Integrity, xxv, 19, 48, 87, 90, 92, 95
  leadership and, 93–94
Intelligence, 73, 74, 78, 79, 90
Interstate School Leaders Licensure Consortium (ISLLC), xxi, 6–7, 8, 9, 43, 59, 61, 62

Journal of Staff Development, 70

Kellner-Rogers, Myron, 22

King, Matthew, 45
Knowledge, 46, 51, 95, 103, 114
Kotter, John, 53, 109–110, 110–111
Kouzes, James, 11, 92

Lambert, Linda, 13–14
Leaders Make It Happen!: An Administrator's Guide to Data Teams (McNulty and Besser), 76–77
Leadership, 35, 61, 62, 65, 74, 75, 77, 97
  assessing, 16–17, 25
  authentic, 55, 89
  behavior of, xxiv, 11, 20
  challenges of, xxvi, 66
  change and, 52, 56, 117
  collaborative, xxi, xxii, 84
  community, 11, 51
  culture and, 42
  defining, 7, 13, 54 (exh.)
  developing, xxi–xxii, 12, 13–14, 17, 43, 48, 117
  effective, xxiv, 4, 10, 81, 108, 111
  ethical dimensions of, 94, 98
  function of, xxiii, xxiv, 68, 101
  integrity and, xxv, 93–94
  learning and, 11, 12, 13, 109
  management and, 52, 53, 54, 55–57, 56 (exh.), 60
  management or, 54–55
  mind/heart/soul of, 4–6, 19
  refocusing, 8, 104, 117
  research of, 6, 14
  responsibility of, xxiv, 18, 21, 22, 24, 25, 26, 99
  roots/wings of, xxii–xxiii, xxv, xxvi, 5, 23
  school, 3, 4, 12, 17–19, 21, 36, 49, 52, 60
  servant, 91–94, 98, 99
  shared, 11, 59, 67, 116
  standards and, xxi, 6, 9, 23–24, 31
  strategy for, 5–6, 113
  success and, 17, 80
  themes for, 7–8
  visionary, 11, 24, 29, 32
Leadership: Theory and Practice, 56
Leadership and Learning Center, The, 61, 66, 75

Leadership for Student Learning: Reinventing the Principalship (IEL), 10–11
Leading Learning Communities: Standards for What Principals Should Know and Be Able To Do (NAESP), 9
Learning, xxi, xxii, 3, 26, 29, 38, 40, 43, 104, 111, 116
  advocating for, xxv–xxvi
  behavior and, 41
  blocks, 63
  chunking, 53
  collaboration and, xxiv–xxv
  commitment to, 42
  curriculum and, 58
  data and, 90
  deep, 27
  difficulty in, 69
  improving, 7, 11, 18, 27, 49, 66, 70, 76–77, 106
  leadership and, 12, 13
  opportunities for, xxv, 82
  professional, 42, 65, 84, 89
  promoting, 25, 52, 96
  responsibility for, 69
  student, xxi, 8, 9, 16, 17, 40, 60, 66, 69, 70, 109
  supporting, 70, 96
  teaching and, 58, 67, 68
  vision of, xxii–xxiii, 22, 23, 72
  why of, 31
Learning by Heart (Barth), 25
Learning community, xxiv, 3, 13, 17, 25, 43, 50, 68, 88, 91, 94
  collaborative, 79, 97
  creating, xxiii, 19, 26, 82
  culture of, 44
  dialogue with, 112
  high-performing, 116
  hope and, 4
  positive, 41, 81
  professional, xxiv, 40, 69–70, 83, 84
Learning environments, xxiv, 63, 64
  effective, 43, 60, 96
Learning Leader, The (Reeves), 28
Learning systems, xxiii–xxiv, 19, 52, 59, 71
Levin, Ben, 111
Lewin, Kurt, 51

Management, 51, 62, 65, 66
  defining, 54 (exh.)
  leadership and, 52, 53, 54, 55–57, 56 (exh.), 60
  leadership or, 54–55
  as process, 54, 54 (exh.)
Mann, Horace, 84, 86
Marzano, Robert, 14
McNulty, Brian, 14, 76–77
Mid-continent Research for Education and Learning (McREL), 14
Mission, 16, 23, 30, 53, 54, 72
Monitoring, 16, 42, 60, 69, 77
Moral purpose, 19, 24, 86, 87, 88–89, 90, 93, 94, 98, 99
Motivation, 39, 48, 53, 72, 82, 84, 107–108
  theory, 77–80
Multipliers, 73, 74, 82, 83
Multipliers: How the Best Leaders Make Everyone Smarter (Wiseman), 73

Nation at Risk, A (National Commission on Excellence in Education), 6, 113, 114
National Association of Elementary School Principals (NAESP), 9, 102
National Association of Secondary School Principals (NASSP), 10
National Center for Education Statistics, 106
National Center for Urban School Transformation, 46
National Commission on Excellence in Education, 6
National Policy Board for Educational Administration (NPBEA), 7
National School Improvement Project, 44
No Child Left Behind Act, 6
Northouse, Peter, 55
  management/leadership and, 56 (exh.)

Organisation for Economic Co-operation and Development (OECD), 105
Organization, xxiii–xxiv, 10, 23, 36, 52, 54, 55, 60

Outcomes, xxvi, 53, 70, 76, 83, 111

Peck, M. Scott, 91
Performance, xxii, xxiii, xxiv, 40, 41, 61, 63, 73, 78, 83, 92, 104, 113, 114
    expectation of, 116
    improving, 71, 88
    leadership, 117
    production and, 58
    standards for, 18
    student, 9, 106
Peters, Tom, 53
Peterson, Kent, 39, 40, 41, 56
Phillips, Gary, 44
Pink, Daniel, 77, 78
Planning teams, 27, 62, 64
Plans, 32, 58, 63, 64
    developing, 23, 55
Policy, xxi, 59, 109, 112, 113
    goals and, 111
Posner, Barry, 11, 92
Principle-Centered Leadership (Covey), 52
Productivity, 39, 58, 74
Programme for International Student Assessment (PISA), 105
Progress, 23, 41, 77
    monitoring/evaluating, 23
Public schools, 85, 105, 112, 113
Purpose, 19, 30, 33, 35

Quality, 40, 88, 103, 114
    access to, 89
    improving, 58–59

Reeves, Douglas, 71, 92, 108
    Data Teams and, 75
    educational leaders and, 16–17
    on vision/action, 28
Reflection, xxii, 13, 18, 35, 71, 89
Reform, 7, 44, 49, 101, 102, 110, 114
    education, 106, 115, 117
    exploring, 114
    initiatives, 58, 117
    school, xxii, 18, 20
Reframing Teacher Leadership (Reeves), 108
Reigeluth, Charles, 111
Relationships, xxiii, 3, 15, 38, 48, 57, 61, 83, 86

cause-and-effect, 36
collaborative, 42
productive, 81
Resiliency, 14, 17, 117
    described, 107–108
Resources, 15, 61, 63, 65, 107
    cultural/social/intellectual, 80
    technological, 60
Respect, 42, 46, 48, 87, 98, 111
Responsibility, 37, 59, 62, 68, 69, 71, 82, 86, 98, 109
    collective, 13, 41
    complex, 52
    honoring, 87
    moral compass and, 99
    strategic, 64
Rewards, 15, 72, 79, 83
Risks, 48–49, 55, 113, 114
    taking, 27, 47, 59, 72, 74

Safety, 38, 60, 63, 103
Saphier, Jon, 45
School culture, xxiii, 36, 37, 39, 43, 45, 46, 65, 71, 87
    healthy, 35, 40, 44, 49, 50
    moral/ethical, 116
    standards for, 48–49
School Leadership That Works (Marzano, Waters, and McNulty), 14
Schooling, xxiv, 19, 36, 90
    moral purpose of, 3, 24, 90
Senge, Peter, 23, 53, 91, 110
Sergiovanni, Thomas, 20, 89, 92
Servant leadership, 91–94, 98, 99
Shaping School Culture: The Heart of Leadership (Deal and Peterson), 39
Skills, 51, 52, 71, 92
    determining, 114
    management, 54, 55, 65, 66
Spears, Larry: on servant leadership, 92–93
Stakeholders, 8, 15, 27, 28, 30, 41, 49, 68, 80, 94
    engaging, 19, 81, 111
    vision and, 33
Standards, xxv, 6, 7, 8, 9, 69, 97
    advocating for, 118
    leadership, xxi, 20
    promoting/communicating, xxiv

Standards *(continued)*
  rigorous, 17
  setting, 104
Strategies, xxii, 28, 36, 49, 68, 110
  leadership, 5–6, 113
  planning/implementation/
    evaluation of, 81
  teaching, 48, 75
Success, xxi, 17, 36, 46, 47, 55, 68, 71, 75, 96, 97
  academic, 12, 90
  celebrating, 40
  challenge of, 28
  contributing to, 18
  ensuring, 91, 117
  exemplars of, 59
  leadership and, 80
  measuring/communicating, 27
  progress and, 41
  promoting, 23, 60, 90, 112
  teaching/learning, 33
Systems change, 111

Teachers, 1, 63
  information for, 62
  retaining, 73
  shortage of, 107
Teaching, xxi, xxii, 26, 29, 38, 65, 82, 103, 116
  changes for, 109
  data and, 90
  effective, 42
  improving, 11, 18, 49, 52, 66, 70, 90, 106
  learning and, 58, 67, 68
  strategies for, 48, 75
  time for, 20
  values/beliefs about, 96
  vision/mission of, 72

Teamwork, 10, 48, 58, 98
Technology, 17, 102, 103, 109
  effective/appropriate, 44
  integrating, xxiv, 63
Total Quality Management (TQM), 58–59, 60, 61, 66
Trends in International Mathematics and Science Study (TIMSS), 105
Trust, xxv, 2, 12, 42, 43, 46, 83, 87
Twain, Mark, xxvi, 21, 67–68, 84, 101, 102
  quote of, 1, 35, 51, 67, 85

Values, 11, 26, 30, 37, 48, 50, 73, 89, 92, 94, 95 (exh.), 96, 98
  cultural, 40
  leadership, 91
  shaping, 99
  shared, 27
Van der Post, Sir Laurens, 3
Vision, xxii, xxv, 3, 11, 12, 16, 18, 29, 50, 52, 54, 72, 94, 116
  action and, 28
  core values and, 30
  developing, 22, 30, 110
  shared, xxiii, 13, 19, 21, 22, 23, 31, 32, 33, 53, 69
  statements, 25–26, 31
  substance/symbols of, 25–28
Vision 2021: Transformations in Leading, Learning and Community (NAESP), 102

Wallace Foundation, 7, 12
Waters, Tim, 14
Welfare, 60, 63, 96, 103
Wheatley, Margaret, 22, 92
Wiseman, Liz, 73, 74